The American History Series
Series Editors
John Hope Franklin, *Duke University*
Abraham S. Eisenstadt, *Brooklyn College*

Arthur S. Link
Princeton University
General Editor for History

Forrest G. Wood
CALIFORNIA STATE COLLEGE, BAKERSFIELD

The Era
of Reconstruction,
1863–1877

Harlan Davidson, Inc.
Arlington Heights, Illinois 60004

ISBN: 0-88295-771-6

(Formerly 0-690-00700-0)

Library of Congress Card Number: 74-13488

Cover illustration: Schomburg Collection, New York Public Library

PRINTED IN THE UNITED STATES OF AMERICA

83 84 85 86 CM9 8 7 6 5 4 3

EDITORS' FOREWORD

Every generation writes its own history, for the reason that it sees the past in the foreshortened perspective of its own experience. This has certainly been true of the writing of American history. The practical aim of our historiography is to offer us a more certain sense of where we are going by helping us understand the road we took in getting where we are. If the substance and nature of our historical writing is changing, it is precisely because our own generation is redefining its direction, much as the generations that preceded us redefined theirs. We are seeking a newer direction, because we are facing new problems, changing our values and premises, and shaping new institutions to meet new needs. Thus, the vitality of the present inspires the vitality of our writing about our past. Today's scholars are hard at work reconsidering every major field of our history: its politics, diplomacy, economy, society, mores, values, sexuality, and status, ethnic, and race relations. No less significantly, our scholars are using newer modes of investigation to probe the ever-expanding domain of the American past.

Our aim, in this American History Series, is to offer the reader a survey of what scholars are saying about the central themes and issues of American history. To present these themes and issues, we have invited scholars who have made notable contributions to the respective fields in which they are writing. Each volume offers the reader a sufficient factual and narrative account for perceiving the larger dimensions of its particular subject. Addressing their respective themes, our authors have undertaken, moreover, to present the conclusions derived by the principal writers on these themes. Beyond that, the authors present their own conclusions about those aspects of their respective subjects that have been matters of difference and controversy. In effect, they have written not only about where the subject stands in today's historiography but also about where they stand on their subject. Each volume closes with an extensive critical essay on the writings of the major authorities on its particular theme.

The books in this series are designed for use in both basic and advanced courses in American history. Such a series has a particular utility in times such as these, when the traditional format of our American history courses is being altered to accommodate a greater diversity of texts and reading materials. The series offers a number of distinct advantages. It extends and deepens the dimensions of course work in American history. In proceeding beyond the confines of the traditional textbook, it makes clear that the study of our past is, more than the student might otherwise infer, at once complex, sophisticated, and profound. It presents American history as a subject of continuing vitality and fresh investigation. The work of experts in their respective fields, it opens up to the student the rich findings of historical inquiry. It invites the student to join, in major fields of research, the many groups of scholars who are pondering anew the central themes and problems of our past. It challenges the student to participate actively in exploring American history and to collaborate in the creative and rigorous adventure of seeking out its wider reaches.

John Hope Franklin

Abraham S. Eisenstadt

CONTENTS

CONTENTS

ONE

Reconstruction and War

WHAT IS RECONSTRUCTION?

The issue of reconstruction did not suddenly appear in 1865 or 1867. Almost as soon as the Civil War began in 1861 there were discussions among government officials and in the press about what postwar America—especially the South—should be like. Nations engaged in war are always faced with postwar adjustment problems, so precedents should not have been hard to find.

But most previous wars had been fought between sovereign nations. In some cases, as in the war with Mexico, a settlement was reached and the loser went its way after paying a tribute. The War of 1812 ended in an apparent stalemate; neither Britain nor the United States gained or lost territory, but a number of far-reaching changes occurred in American life as a result of the war. The War for American Independence ended when the thirteen colonies, in effect seceding from the British Empire, finally persuaded the English government to give up trying to force them back. Nor were there precedents for a postwar settlement in previous European wars. In the distant past various nation-states conquered other nation-states and assimilated them, and in some cases—such as the Roman Empire—made them like it. But this sort of thing was too far removed from the American experience to provide much of a lesson.

There was, in short, no example of postwar adjustment that government leaders could look to because there had been no war to compare with the American Civil War. Even civil wars elsewhere produced few lessons because their geographical and social circumstances differed so greatly. Those wars, such as the English Civil War in the seventeenth century, had usually been between rival political groups struggling for control of a relatively homogeneous society. But the American Civil War was a war of secession. In many respects, the South *was* a separate nation in more than just name. The Confederate States of America, representing a distinct geographical region with unique political, economic, social, and intellectual institutions, was fighting for a way of life that evidently was not compatible with the rest of American society. A northern victory meant the end of that fight. In theory, the nation would once again be whole, but such a supposition was hard to sustain because the nation had never been whole in the first place. Perhaps the basic difficulty involving reconstruction was that the two regions had always had enduring cultural differences.

There may not have been two sovereign nations struggling over an international dispute, but there were certainly two sides fighting in battles that were among the bloodiest in human history. There was going to be a winner and a loser, and slogans about charity for all and malice towards none would not change that fact. The victorious federal government was sure to demand a major role in restoring the defeated South to some kind of "reasonable" status. To have allowed the South to restore itself would have virtually guaranteed a return to many of the same conditions that had led to the war in the first place.

But what should that restoration consist of? More to the point, what kind of postwar nation should emerge from all this?

Some of the answers to these questions were dictated by the circumstances of the war itself. Slavery was dead; the national government certainly would not permit any attempt to reestablish it. The war also eliminated secession as an effective alternative in settling sectional disputes. But these answers only led to more questions. Since slavery would not be reestablished, what should be the nature of the relationship between the races in the South—or in the whole country, for that matter? Could one expect the South to treat the freedmen the same way the North treated its black population (which left a lot to be desired) when the sheer weight of numbers in the South was so much greater? Did the government that freed the slaves actually have a clear responsibility to go beyond emancipation, to lift up four million people who were the victims of two and a half centuries of racist oppression? To an enlightened twentieth-century generation, the answer is clearly yes. But in the nineteenth century such an action would surely lead to a national encroachment into prerogatives traditionally claimed by the states. How could the citizens of the defeated South believe they were free and equal if in fact their rights, as they defined them, were being denied by the victors? It was obvious that some very great and very difficult decisions had to be made.

As for other fundamental changes that the war was sure to bring, many of them were already well under way. By borrowing heavily to pay for the war, the national government set a precedent for all future wars. Under the provisions of the National Banking Act of 1863 and its amendments, financiers like Jay Cooke were building an enormous pool of investment capital that was to become the foundation of the great postwar economic surge. For whatever that was worth, an unfortunate consequence was the inflation that accentuated the disparity between wage-earners and the more prosperous segments of the population; a development that, in turn, contributed to the later efforts to organize labor on a national scale. In manufacturing, small industries such as ready-made clothing and meat-packing were growing to full-scale production for a mass market. At an international trade exposition in Paris in 1867, American industrial precision tools and an American locomotive were judged to be the finest, a sharp contrast to their showing at a similar exposition in 1855. In the country, farmers were adjusting to the manpower shortage by shifting rapidly to mechanical devices, making the American farmer the most technological in the world, but at the same time laying the foundation for what was to become agriculture's chronic problem: overproduction. The country was changing.

WHO SHALL DECIDE?

Probably the first question that had to be answered was just which branch of the national government would have the primary authority in defining the terms of reconstruction, a question that quickly became entangled in legal complexities. The Constitution, of course, made no provision for disunion and therefore none for reunion. There were, however, certain implied alternatives which, unfortunately, were subject to varying interpretations. Since a war was involved, did not this give the president, as commander-in-chief of the army of occupation, the power to complete the process? On the other hand, should not the Congress, acting on the grounds that the war was strictly a domestic conflict and involved no treaty-making matters, initiate legislation outlining the terms of reconstruction? A third but remote possibility was that the national government might simply withdraw its military forces and allow the southern states to reorganize as they wished and send whomever they choose to

Congress. If the eleven seceded states rescinded their secession ordinances and affirmed their loyalty to the United States, was there any reason to deny them full restoration?

Indeed, the initial reconstruction policy discussed in government circles at the beginning of the war was simply one of restoring the seceded states with their powers intact. At that time, it was considered crucial not to alienate the loyal slave states—especially Kentucky, which was precariously close to declaring for the Confederacy—so no conditions that would have been repugnant to them were publicly discussed. Setting conditions would also have been an open challenge to the principle of states' rights, which was still held dear by most Southerners. It was not until well along in the war and after the border states of Missouri, Kentucky, Maryland, and Delaware were unequivocally committed to the union cause that federal authorities could risk a discussion of stringent reconstruction guidelines.

The controversy over who had the power to reconstruct was further complicated by a disagreement over the legality of secession. The southern leadership, some congressional Republicans contended, had abdicated its rightful authority when it led the South out of the Union. The basis of this argument was that a state committed suicide when it seceded and therefore no longer existed. Not being foreign lands, the former Confederate states were subject to congressional legislation. Obviously, there were contradictions in this argument. Some of the same people who were saying this now had said earlier that secession was illegal, that a state was indestructible and therefore could not leave the Union. But if the states were still states, the Congress could not treat them like territories. The only job at hand would be to reestablish normal relations between the state and national governments. This would be done by disfranchising the secession leaders and requiring the election of men who would profess their loyalty to the United States. Nothing more, nothing less. Abraham Lincoln's reconstruction policies were essentially based on this principle. Although his program did not go so far as to give a free hand to the southern state governments, and he demanded the inclusion of emancipation, his main intent was to restore the South to its "normal" condition as quickly and with as little fuss as possible.

Despite the fact that the territorial theory implied an *ex post facto* recognition of the Confederacy, many Republican congressmen considered it compelling. They contended, as historian Herman Belz pointed out in *Reconstructing the Union: Theory and Policy during the Civil War* (1969), that the secessionists had caused the "legal and constitutional destruction of the states and reduced them to territories." This amounted to a "practical abdication" and "instant forfeiture" of all ordinary state powers, Republican leaders like John Bingham and Charles Sumner reasoned, and therefore a seceded state "lapsed" into a territory. Furthermore, the decision of the Supreme Court in the *Prize Cases* (1863) in which the Court, by a five-to-four vote, upheld the president's right to initiate war measures prior to the congressional recognition of an insurrection (July 13, 1861), supported the forfeiture argument. But because of the closeness of the vote, and with the chief justice leading the dissent, the decision also reflected the conflict and portended the struggle to come.

What eventually emerged in decisions handed down by the Supreme Court was what could be called a double-status theory, as set forth in *Miller* v. *U.S.* (1871). The Court had no jurisdiction over foreign matters, therefore any action on its part proceeded from the assumption that the secession was illegal. But such an assumption could hamper certain military operations, such as establishing a blockade of southern ports. Under the double-status theory the national government declared the Confederacy a belligerent, which was little more than a recognition of the fact that the southern states were engaged in an armed rebellion against the United States. In the last analysis, the Court facilitated the prosecution of the war, but it did nothing to resolve the conflict over who had the power to reconstruct.

If the controversy over reconstruction could have been confined to a constitutional dialogue, some of the subsequent difficulties might have been avoided. But that was asking too much. As early as the summer of 1862 the conflict began to shift to a power struggle between the Congress and the president. It needs to be remembered that Republican militants had first emerged during the darkest moments of the Civil War when certain congressmen criticized Lincoln for not pursuing a more vigorous war policy. Thus the radical faction was born as an opposition force, opposing the president and opposing anyone who favored a conciliatory posture toward the South. Although the radicals in Congress were clearly in the minority, their ranks included a number of veteran abolitionists; thus they brought to the political stage a tenacity and vituperative aggressiveness that was difficult to ignore. In addition, they occupied some of the key committee chairmanships, so their number was not a true measure of their influence. Moreover, there were a number of moderate Republicans who agreed with the president's policies but who nonetheless insisted that the Congress had a right to legislate the matter. The main points of contention were the reorganizing of the southern state governments, the calling for elections, and the readmission of the southern representatives to the Congress. Although the war was still in progress and its prosecution was clearly a presidential responsibility, postwar reconstruction, in the minds of a growing number of congressional Republicans, was a domestic issue and therefore subject to legislation.

Moreover, most of the president's critics considered the wartime reconstruction efforts as only temporary arrangements that would be set aside for a uniform procedure established for the entire South after the shooting had stopped. There were more than a few senators and congressmen who were anxious for the war to end so that they could get on to the job of implementing their policies unhindered by the president's military priority. Thus it became a waiting game. It also should not be forgotten that Lincoln never denied that Congress should have a role in reconstruction. On numerous occasions he pointed out that the responsibility for seating representatives and senators rested solely in each house. This inferred, of course, that the Congress could express its displeasure with reconstruction by simply refusing to seat members-elect from the seceded states—which was eventually what happened in 1865. Such an action, admittedly, did not give the Congress the power to initiate policy or influence directly the reorganization of the southern state governments. Once Lincoln got wind of the thinking among Republican congressional leaders, he hoped to retain the initiative so as to head off a settlement that, in his view, was certain to produce bitterness, disillusionment, and even bloodshed.

In addition to the factors already mentioned, there were several other reasons for the growing congressional aggressiveness. First, some Republicans favored "complete and thorough" reconstruction because it appeared to be the best way of guaranteeing the ascendancy of their party. If the southern blacks could be mobilized into a unified voting bloc, they could assure a Republican majority in the Congress for years to come. As one revisionist historian, Kenneth M. Stampp, in *The Era of Reconstruction, 1865–1877* (1965), observed, "Thaddeus Stevens . . . once frankly admitted that he had a political motive." Second, northern business and financial interests also had a stake in such an outcome. Many merchants and industrialists feared that the southern states would send to the Congress the same kind of men who had dominated their previous delegations. The result could be the repeal of the various wartime economic measures favorable to manufacturing and commerce. These two reasons, both of which carried the onus of selfishness, have been commonly set forth by traditional historians as the primary bases of congressional reconstruction. But the modern concern for civil rights and human equality has called attention to a third and more compelling reason. Genuine reformers saw reconstruction as an opportunity to bring about a social revolution, an opportunity to elevate the black race that almost certainly would not be repeated in their lifetimes, if ever. Reconstruction offered the American people a chance to redeem themselves for two and a half centuries of chattel slavery. This humanitarian motive, clearly set forth in Hans L. Trefousse's

The Radical Republicans: Lincoln's Vanguard for Racial Justice (1969), contrasts sharply with the motives considered in older accounts.

THE PRESIDENT ACTS

As long as the war continued, Lincoln retained the upper hand in determining reconstruction procedures. As soon as the army had secured a state, and sometimes before, the president would appoint a military governor whose main task would be to supervise the orderly return of civil authority. Lincoln named Andrew Johnson as military governor of Tennessee in 1862, and a civil government, with federal military aid, functioned continuously thereafter, although Confederate forces in the state were not subdued until the fall of 1863. During this period the president could dictate many of the terms under which a state would be reorganized.

By December 1862, Lincoln had established a procedure that he hoped would test the waters and become a pattern for the reconstruction of the other southern states. While the state government of Louisiana was still under military control, army officials supervised the election of two congressmen, Michael Hahn and Benjamin Flanders. Since Congress made the rules under which members are seated, Lincoln's action was, in effect, an acknowledgement of at least partial congressional responsibility. He could have played it safe and moved to reorganize the state government first, and thereby avoid congressional interference. Somewhat unexpectedly, the House of Representatives seated the two new members. Although he was to endure later opposition, this action was the most important test to date of Lincoln's policy and it was clearly a victory.

There were, of course, other elements involved in the Louisiana situation. By welcoming the state's national representatives back into the federal family before the state government itself had been reorganized, the notion that the state had never really been out of the Union was reinforced. The action also served as an object lesson to the white citizens of Louisiana—

and, by inference, to the entire white South—that the national government intended to be fair and generous, and that they should therefore support efforts to organize a loyal state government. Probably most important of all, in the long view, was the presentation of reconstruction as an accomplished fact. Although Lincoln conceded that his efforts were in large measure tentative, he was also aware that the more slowly reconstruction progressed the greater role the Congress would demand. Ideally, if each state could be at least partially reconstructed on the Louisiana model, there would be little left to do when the fighting ended except replace the military officials with responsible civil authorities. The course of action followed in Louisiana was designed to produce results that the Congress would have no choice but to accept.

But if speed was the most important thing, there was a price to pay for it—and here a modern civil libertarian is tempted to question Lincoln's priorities. Presidential reconstruction may have expedited the return of peace and tranquility, but for whom? Surely, not for the former slaves whose status of perpetual subservience would be anything but peaceful and tranquil. It was clear that the kind of shortcuts Lincoln called for would raise questions about the legitimacy, and even the loyalty, of the new southern state governments. Basically, the president's requirements for reconstruction were simple. All a southern candidate for office had to do was renounce slavery and secession and declare his loyalty to the United States. A representative so elected would be chosen only by white male voters, and then by only a fraction of them. By denying the freedmen a political voice Lincoln could be accused of acquiescing in bigotry. How much of this charge could the president justify on the grounds of expediency? In answering this question, we must remind ourselves of both the uniqueness and reality of the situation. Lincoln was striving for what he thought was achievable. If there were injustices, as he probably suspected there would be, they would have to be corrected later. Otherwise, there would be no settlement at all.

Besides Louisiana, a reconstruction precedent of sorts was

established with the admission, in 1863, of the state of West Virginia. The residents of the northwestern corner of Virginia had long had sharp disagreements with the eastern counties. With an economic and social orientation toward the Old Northwest instead of the South, western Virginians had complained of many of the problems that had been common in states that had a sparsely populated backcountry and an older, established eastern seaboard: economic discrimination, unfair taxation, disproportionate representation, and so on. While there was no way of determining precisely what percentage of the people in this area opposed secession, it was clear that a majority did so in most of the fifty counties that became the new state. There were, to be sure, several irregularities in the defection of the counties. It appeared, for example, that the unionists who led the new state movement represented only a portion of the counties for which they professed to speak.

The West Virginia case is also a good example of the kind of question over which historians are bound to disagree. It was argued by James G. Randall and David Donald in *The Civil War and Reconstruction* (2d ed., 1961) that, because of the absence of negotiation with the rest of Virginia and because there was no constitutional or statutory provision for state division, the creation of West Virginia was illegal. On the face of it, this was true. But the action also underscored the questionable legality of much of what was being done during this period. The process by which West Virginia was created was, in fact, no more illegal than the process by which the Richmond Convention of April 17, 1861, professing to speak for all Virginians, had seceded. Indeed, one can even justify the creation of West Virginia as the way in which some of Virginia's citizens resisted the illegal act of secession. Whatever its legality, it worked.

While the separate efforts at reconstruction in Louisiana and West Virginia, and to a lesser extent in Tennessee, made some headway, the fact remained that as late as the fall of 1863 there was no general reconstruction policy for the South as a whole. What seemed to be suitable for one state was not necessarily feasible for another. Social and economic circumstances varied; and as long as military operations took precedence, there would always be compelling pressures that made each state's reconstruction an *ad hoc* affair. But as the area under federal occupation continued to grow and the end of the war came into clearer focus, and with the radical Republicans in Congress growing more aggressive, reconstruction was becoming a major issue. The president could not continue to bide his time indefinitely and retain the initiative. The result was the announcement of the "10 percent" plan.

On December 8, 1863, Lincoln issued a Proclamation of Amnesty and Reconstruction in which he laid down the terms of his program for the restoration of the South. There was a strong undertone of wartime expediency in the program, and Lincoln did not consider it the final solution to the problem, but it did, nonetheless, clarify the situation considerably and it could stand as a compelling precedent for the future. The first of the plan's two major provisions was complete amnesty for all Southerners who had taken active part in the rebellion, except certain former high-ranking Confederate military and civil officers. Those eligible needed only to take an oath of allegiance to the United States and to agree to obey all federal laws and proclamations. They would then be entitled to vote for state officers and their property rights would be fully restored (excepting slaves). The second part of the proclamation spelled out the terms under which a seceded state could be fully restored to the Union. As soon as a number of citizens in a state equal to one-tenth of the total votes cast in that state in the presidential election of 1860 was registered, those registered could act to reestablish a state government. Moreover, the state and local election laws already in existence would continue in force. While this stipulation was included ostensibly to minimize confusion, it meant, of course, that blacks would not vote. Nor did these voters have a completely free hand in reorganizing their governments; their actions must comply with federal laws and proclamations; in particular, they had to recognize emancipation. This done, the president would recognize the state as being fully restored.

The Lincoln plan had something for both conservatives,

who thought the national government should have little or no role in dictating reconstruction, and the radicals, who advocated "complete and thorough" reconstruction, though it satisfied neither completely. The general amnesty provision was based largely on the premise that the use of the pardoning power, as Herman Belz pointed out, "was consistent with the conservative view of the war as a rebellion of individuals against their government." A whole people should not be punished for the rash conduct of certain individuals. Moreover, the action was conciliatory in tone, an attempt "to bind up the nation's wounds," as it were. However, the language and substance of both the proclamation and the annual message to Congress that accompanied it also suggested strongly an agreement with the radical contention that the seceded states had committed suicide, and that there was indeed far more to reconstruction than merely reestablishing state governments. The basic radical premise, that the federal government should set the terms of restoration, was intrinsic to the plan, and the reactions of several leading radicals in the Congress were generally favorable. Because of these implications, it is a distortion of the 10 percent plan to think of it in terms of its leniency, as so many historians have done. It only appeared lenient when compared to some of the radical proposals.

A further analysis showed that a central element of Lincoln's program was his concern for those Southerners who had opposed secession from the start and who presumably still believed in the cause of union. Throughout the war there were pockets of unionist loyalty in the South, e.g., eastern Tennessee. This led optimistic Northerners to conclude that there were many Southerners who were anxious to profess their unionism, but who remained silent for fear of reprisals. Lincoln was not moved to launch a general reconstruction program until he was convinced that the unionists within each southern state were not going to act, as they had in Virginia. When he finally did announce his plan, he made it as easy as he could for them to come to the fore by requiring that only one-tenth of the electorate be active. In this respect the 10 percent plan was clearly a wartime measure because it was designed to enable the loyal minority to win control of a state while the secessionist element was in disarray and the federal army was present.

(But the president overestimated the strength of southern unionism. The simple truth was that the vast majority of white Southerners supported the Confederate government, though not all with the same enthusiasm and many simply because it was the judicious thing to do. Indeed, though few of them had been plantation owners, most of them fought for the "cause" with an almost religious zeal. It was perhaps one of the greatest hoaxes in human history that as many as a million men were persuaded to defend a "way of life" the benefits of which they would never share. The tradition of deference was strong in the South. Moreover, many rebel soldiers were simple folk who clung to the illusion that they would someday be slaveowners. The realities of the situation should have made it clear that few of them would ever attain that status. But at the same time, for the president to wait for a unionist emergence in the South was equally unrealistic.

The Lincoln plan also had a long-range political objective: to establish a permanent, viable Republican party in the South. As Kenneth M. Stampp pointed out, Lincoln never lost sight of the political opportunity that reconstruction offered. It was the president's hope to win over to Republican ranks as many old southern Whigs as possible. Himself a former Whig, Lincoln must have sympathized with these men without a party. Not only had they been a significant opposition to the Democrats before the war, but they had included in their ranks a disproportionately large number of wealthy planters. The northern Democrats had made it clear, as early as the elections of 1862, that the Republican majority in the Congress was precarious. Most leading Republicans were convinced that it was essential to the party's future to win southern support or forever be a sectional, and therefore minority, party. It was Lincoln's view that this could best be done—perhaps only be done—by bringing into the Republican fold the 40 percent of the white voters of the South who would otherwise drift to the Democrats. The Republican party must not lose control by default.

Moreover, it made good political sense to be charitable. The hard-line, punitive approach urged by the radicals might produce some immediate short-term gains, but they would only be temporary and they would surely lay seeds of resistance among southern whites. Republican strength in the South would be far more enduring, Lincoln was convinced, if it was achieved by positive means. Such glowing phrases as "bind up the nation's wounds" and "malice toward none and charity for all" were not merely examples of the president's benevolence, but were also the carefully chosen words of a shrewd politician. Something many Americans have tended to overlook in their adulation of Lincoln is that he was one of the cleverest politicians ever to occupy the White House. He was also realistic enough to understand that many white Southerners would be so embittered by losing the war that no amount of wooing would win them over. But he was convinced that an alternative must be offered to those voters who had traditionally opposed the Democratic party.

In contrast to Lincoln, the radicals believed that the white Southerners would be incorrigible and that the only way to ensure a permanent Republican party in the South was to *force* it through suffrage for the freedmen. It was this very element of coercion that Lincoln believed would guarantee failure; he believed that southern whites might, if handled tenderly, voluntarily share the ballot box with the freedmen. And even if they did not, the loss of black suffrage was a small price to pay for an established Republican party in the South. It is easy to criticize Lincoln for ignoring the interests of the freedmen, but this was Lincoln the political realist. He was convinced that permanent political stability and racial harmony could never be established in the South without the cooperation of the white leadership. The southern whites were, after all, a majority in most of the South; they still possessed most of the wealth and property; and the habit and tradition of leadership was theirs. With the education, the experience, the economic control, and the tradition of authority, they could not be ignored in any reconstruction plan. One of the greatest mistakes that the radicals made was to minimize the importance of the old southern leadership.

The radicals argued that there was much more to reconstruction than just establishing the Republican party in the South. To begin with, who was going to pay the enormous costs of the war? From July 1861, to March 1865, the national government incurred a loan debt of over 2.6 billion dollars. Was there no indemnity due? Moreover, the heaviest costs were not those measured in dollars. Homes, lives, and businesses were being turned upside down. By the end of the war over 360,000 northern soldiers and sailors would have lost their lives (although less than a third of them died from battle wounds). Thousands more were being injured and maimed (although this was to become the trademark of many successful postwar political careers as opportunists, like Lucius Fairchild of Wisconsin who always campaigned with his empty sleeve prominently displayed, vigorously waved the "bloody shirt"). Somebody had to pay for all this. Should those responsible be let off with nothing more than a slap on the wrist? The radical Republicans wanted not merely to punish the secessionists, but to prevent them from reestablishing their political leadership of the southern states. Surely, they would send to the Congress the same men, or the same kinds of men, who had walked out of it in 1861. At the least, the radicals felt, these men should never be allowed to govern again. Their answer to the president's plan was the Wade-Davis bill.

THE CONGRESS REACTS

In February 1864, Representative Henry Winter Davis of Maryland introduced House Bill 244, which was to become the focal point of the anti-Lincoln forces. The bill called for the presidential appointment of a civil governor in each former Confederate state who would administer all laws until a permanent state government was established. Each state was to repudiate its war debt, making those who had financed the southern military effort the big losers and enabling the new state government to get started without an enormous deficit. The bill further declared all slaves "forever free," and the federal courts were directed to issue writs of *habeas corpus* against anyone who deprived a freedman of his liberty, a measure which constituted a far-reaching change in nation-state relationships. But, as with the president's plan, Davis's proposal was based on white suffrage only, and it permitted the calling of a constitutional convention after only one-tenth of all white voters enrolled had taken an oath to support the United States Constitution.

It was at this point that the Davis bill departed sharply from the Lincoln plan. To be eligible to vote for delegates to a constitutional convention one must, after already having pledged to support the United States Constitution, take an "iron-clad" oath in which he swore that he had never borne arms against the United States or aided the rebellion, a requirement that could disfranchise a substantial portion of the southern population. Thus, while the Lincoln oath was a pledge of future loyalty, the Davis oath demanded a test of past allegiance, or at least neutrality. Moreover, all Confederate and state officials, both civil and military, would be stripped of their citizenship.

By the time the bill passed the House of Representatives in May by a 73 to 59 vote, two important amendments had been added representing concessions by each side. The most far-reaching change raised from 10 to 50 percent the minimum number of enrolled voters taking the oath to support the Constitution. Whatever the intent behind this change, it would almost certainly postpone the completion of reconstruction until the war was over and therefore weaken the role of the president. As long as only one-tenth of the voters had been required to take the oath, the unionists in a state could conceivably reorganize their government while the war was still in progress, an idea that Lincoln encouraged. But requiring a majority made this impossible. Although the radicals were not the only ones who favored the change, it did slow the reconstruction process and thus appealed to those who opposed the president. The second amendment simply removed from the list of those who would lose their citizenship all southern officials below certain ranks. This was supposed to mollify Democrats and moderate Republicans because it protected the citizenship of a significant portion of the traditional southern leadership. Since the most influential secessionists were in the higher positions, they would not be affected by the change. (Though the Davis bill has been described by some historians as a harsh and punitive measure, a careful analysis of the bill passed by the House of Representatives shows it to be quite restrained in most of its terms and not extreme in any of them except for the "iron-clad" oath. Indeed, some radicals criticized it as too lenient, while others supported it only because it was the best that could be had.)

In the Senate the Davis bill was referred to the Committee on Territories chaired by Benjamin F. Wade of Ohio. For reasons not entirely known, Wade, after adding amendments, let the bill languish for several weeks. Meanwhile, the Republican party, calling itself the Union party, held its presidential nominating convention in Baltimore and renominated Lincoln by acclamation. Following the convention, the head-spinning progress of what was now the Wade-Davis bill must have had veteran Congress watchers rubbing their eyes in disbelief. When the bill finally came to the floor of the Senate on July 1, Wade's most significant amendment was the removal of the white-only qualification for voting. Here was a step that could have become a landmark in the history of civil rights in the United States. But it was too much for the other senators. With Wade himself yielding to the racism of his colleagues, they threw the amendment out, 24 to 5. They then voted 17 to 16 to substitute their own, entirely different, reconstruction bill and sent it to the House where it was rejected. But before the matter could be handed over to a conference committee where a compromise would be worked out, the Senate, in one of the most bizarre moves ever made in the Congress, voted to withdraw its own bill and passed, 18 to 14, the *original* bill passed by the House of

Representatives in May. As matters turned out, Wade's name does not even really belong on the bill, let alone be placed first. The next move was the president's.

Wade's decision not to act quickly on the Davis bill may have been what killed it. Had Lincoln received it sooner, he would have been faced with the choice of signing or vetoing it; and had he chosen the latter, he would have assured a direct confrontation with the radicals. Wade apparently did not rush the bill through his committee because he was confident the president would sign it. While it was being debated in the House, Lincoln had not shown any sign of opposition. Thus when he indicated in the final days of the session that he was not going to sign the bill, the radicals were surprised. The Constitution specifies that a bill not returned to the Congress within ten days automatically becomes law unless the Congress is not in session to receive it, in which case the measure is dead. The pocket veto method of getting rid of undesirable legislation by doing nothing had not been a common practice before Lincoln's time. Only a few presidents since Lincoln have used it with any frequency, and no president had ever used it before Andrew Jackson. There still seems to be an odious element of evasion in a pocket veto. It would appear to be more honest for a president to clarify his position with an outright veto.

But a veto can also be more dangerous. It is usually accompanied by an explanation of objections. Under the circumstances that prevailed in the summer of 1864, a presidential criticism of a congressional proposal would have stirred up arguments within the party that could hurt its candidates in the fall elections. Moreover, to veto the bill after appearing neutral toward it during its course through the Congress would have been interpreted by some Republicans as a betrayal. Lincoln had no desire to antagonize moderates and strengthen the Congress's resolve to oppose him, as Andrew Johnson was to do later. In light of the final vote for the bill in each house, it was unlikely a veto could have been overridden, but the stigma of betrayal would have lingered, impairing the president's already strained relations with the Congress. In remaining silent, at least

Lincoln was not giving the radicals anything specific for which he could later be called to task. No president has ever found the pocket veto attractive, but Lincoln considered the Wade-Davis bill unacceptable and a pocket veto was the least offensive way of getting rid of it.

A short time after Congress adjourned, Lincoln tried to cool the rising radical anger by issuing a curious proclamation in which he stated that the procedure outlined in the Wade-Davis bill, though it had not become law, could be adopted by any seceded state that *chose* to follow it. His major criticism of the bill was not its restrictive features, he said, but its commitment to a single, inflexible method. What was good for one state might not be suitable for another. In effect, Lincoln was advocating a dual reconstruction program (with an implication that still other plans might be acceptable). Moreover, there were certain problems that troubled him deeply. Louisiana and Arkansas had already written new constitutions and had reorganized their governments under the president's 10 percent plan. There was no provision in the Wade-Davis bill exempting them. Since both states would have had to scrap their efforts and start all over again under new rules, Lincoln did not think it would be fair to those unionists who had acted in good faith. It can also be argued that the president was trying to ensure party harmony on the eve of an election, but the proclamation pacified few of his critics. Faced with a choice between the Lincoln plan and the Wade-Davis plan, a seceded state would not find it difficult to decide which one to take.

While the president's proclamation did nothing to appease the radicals, there was little they could do as long as the Congress was recessed. Trying to keep the issue alive, Davis and Wade, in their so-called manifesto, condemned Lincoln for his pocket veto and strongly asserted the Congress's "paramount" right to establish reconstruction policies. Although, as historian Herman Belz has explained in *Reconstructing the Union: Theory and Policy during the Civil War* (1969), the Wade-Davis Manifesto was conceived in an effort to defeat Lincoln's reelection bid, it was also a focal point for radical bitterness and an accurate summary of the Congress's opinion of its authority. A number of moderate Republicans in the Congress, such as Isaac Arnold and Henry Dawes, had opposed a hard-line reconstruction program but had voted for the Wade-Davis bill because they believed that Congress had the right to legislate on the matter. Additionally, the Manifesto was a surprisingly accurate forecast of the reconstruction measures that would be drawn up by the Congress in the years following the war. It should, therefore, be best remembered for its significance as a radical Republican policy statement on reconstruction rather than for its political aim. Its angry tone, however, created sympathy for the president, so it failed in that respect.

Students of reconstruction history should resist the temptation to think of the Lincoln and Wade-Davis plans only in terms of their contrast. In the last analysis, a comparison of the two shows more similarities than differences. In a sense, Lincoln was moving more to the left than was the Congress, within the context of their original positions. Republicans who had first advocated a complete overhaul of the southern states modified their views in a less radical direction; Lincoln, who originally wanted quick restoration with few conditions, gradually moved towards a more revolutionary position. What had happened, in effect, was that the president and the Congress started at opposite poles and began moving toward the center, but never really met.

EMANCIPATION

Further clouding the reconstruction picture was the status of four million black people in the South. Despite the Emancipation Proclamation, the matter of their freedom was far from settled by the end of the war. Motivated partly by military expediency, Lincoln had declared free only those slaves who, on January 1, 1863, were in those parts of the South still in rebellion. In truth, some slaves had been emancipated in the first year of the war as a result of the Confiscation Act of August 6,

1861, which called for the freeing of any captured slaves who had been used for Confederate military purposes. Because of the efforts of some racist army commanders to return slaves to their owners and Lincoln's early desire to evade the issue, far fewer slaves were probably freed under this act and its companion law of July 17, 1862, than the measures permitted. On the other hand, of the approximately 180,000 black men who had served in the northern army, the majority had been recruited in occupied areas of the South with the promise of freedom for their service. Thus slaves were being freed by one means or another almost from the beginning of the war.

But that was part of the problem. Because slaves had acquired their freedom so many different ways, and because there were still many slaves who did not qualify under any of the existing categories, there was a great deal of confusion over the status of the black population as a whole, especially in the loyal slave states where the Emancipation Proclamation had never applied. Moreover, since the proclamation had been a wartime measure, did it apply in peacetime to those areas of the South that had never been occupied or to those areas already under federal control before its announcement? There simply was no uniform policy of law that applied to blacks everywhere. West Virginia's new state constitution of 1863 had mandated gradual emancipation; and by early 1865, both Missouri and Maryland had abolished slavery. But Delaware and Kentucky refused to go along, the latter opposing even compensated emancipation; and their state governments continued to claim that slavery was legal, despite the presence of federal soldiers, which made the enforcement of their slave codes difficult. Tennessee was the first former Confederate state to abolish slavery when, in February 1865, it passed a constitutional amendment calling for immediate emancipation. But, as could be expected, this piecemeal approach to emancipation only added to the confusion.

The uncertainty was magnified by the fear among many Northerners that the southern planters would try to reduce their former slaves to a state of peonage scarcely removed from slavery. Left to themselves with only state and local laws to restrain them, the members of the old planter oligarchy would find it easy to comply with the letter of the Emancipation Proclamation while undermining its intent. In short, it became obvious even before the end of the war that a constitutional amendment would be imperative to remove unequivocally and forever all doubts about the existence of slavery in the United States. Accordingly, in April 1864, the Senate passed a resolution that was to become the Thirteenth Amendment. To a generation that launched the modern civil rights movement of the twentieth century, the adoption of a law guaranteeing the basic freedom of four million people would appear to be a fairly simple task. Indeed, when viewed alongside the Fourteenth and Fifteenth Amendments, the Thirteenth has almost always attracted less attention because its conception and passage appeared to be a routine matter. But this was far from the case. It was not until after the elections of 1864 had jolted the membership into action that the House of Representatives, failing once to get the necessary two-thirds majority, finally approved the amendment on January 31, 1865.

There were several reasons for the resistance. To begin with, strict constructionists had doubts about the use of the amending process to effect what they considered an act of social reform. In the mid-nineteenth century, many Americans simply believed that moral issues were not the proper concerns of government. Moreover, while the dogma of states' rights had taken a beating in the previous decade, there were still many conservative Americans who did not believe that property defined by a state was a subject for national government attention. Furthermore, some of these same people viewed the application of national power to a matter involving only some of the states as an unwarranted usurpation of authority over a local institution. Many people also wondered if the Constitution could be amended at all when eleven of the states that would be called upon to ratify the amendment were not organized to do so, or simply refused. The seceded states accounted for more than one-fourth of all the states of the Union; it would be impossible to ratify a constitutional amendment without the support of some of them. On the other hand, if the states of the old Confederacy were not considered to be in the Union, then they would not be counted among the total states. The fact that the Congress did not recognize the state governments in the South but that the administration accepted the ratification of the Thirteenth Amendment of eight of them was one of the many paradoxes of the reconstruction era.

Nor was there agreement within the Republican party on the question of emancipation. In mid-1864, William Seward and Thurlow Weed had questioned the wisdom of making emancipation a term of surrender. Of course, this could have been a practical decision based on the premise that the Confederacy would be less inclined to surrender if it was faced with an obnoxious demand, but their position could also be attributed to their racism. It was the "dark, deep-rooted prejudice of race," LaWanda and John H. Cox wrote in *Politics, Principle, and Prejudice, 1865–1866: Dilemma of Reconstruction America* (1963), that lay behind the opposition of many Democrats to the Thirteenth Amendment. For over two centuries, white racism had been one of the most pervasive factors in American life. It would be naive to think that most Republicans did not share this prejudice just because they were Republicans.

TWO

Congressional Reconstruction

THE HONEYMOON

In March 1865, the Congress created the Bureau of Refugees, Freedmen and Abandoned Lands, commonly called the Freedmen's Bureau. Set up under the War Department, the bureau was headed by General Oliver O. Howard, and it had as its primary mission the care and welfare of the thousands of Southerners, white and black, whose lives had been uprooted by the war. Being without precedent, the bureau was one of the most important agencies of the Civil War era. With branches in every southern state, it established free schools and hospitals, relocated refugees under the provisions of the Homestead Act, distributed millions of food rations, provided legal assistance, operated as an employment agency, negotiated contracts for workers (making it the first national arbitration agency between labor and capital), and otherwise worked to facilitate the former slave's adjustment to his new status. The bureau was originally established to last just one year after the end of the war, but it was obvious that its services would be needed much longer.

The bureau was called the "Freedmen's Bureau" for good reason. Although it was created to serve whites as well as blacks, most whites eschewed its services. The vast majority of those whites who were eligible for aid had been poor before the war, kept that way largely by a slave system that depressed wages for free men and discouraged enterprise. Asking the Freedmen's Bureau for help now would have been, in their minds, tantamount to admitting social equality with blacks. Because of this, and because, after Johnson began handing out wholesale pardons to former rebels and allowing southern planters to repossess their estates, there was little abandoned land to dispose of, the bureau devoted itself mainly to the care and welfare of the former slaves. Accordingly, whites in both North and South came to consider service to the freedmen its exclusive function.

Until recently, that is how historians have also tended to portray the Freedmen's Bureau. For years the most popular view of the bureau, like the traditional view of reconstruction, was the view held by its critics, mostly white Southerners. The bureau was hated. It was run by the military and was therefore a conspicuous agent of an army of occupation. As a constant reminder of defeat in war, it was especially hard for a society with strong cavalier traditions to accept. Because some bureau officials used their positions for personal gain, critics were quick to accuse the entire organization of graft and corruption; thus the worst side of its activities was magnified through countless northern Democratic and southern newspaper editorials. For this reason, historians have tended to see the Freedmen's Bureau in terms of its impact on *white* society, particularly how it was hated and resisted. As late as 1955, the major study of the bureau, George R. Bentley's *A History of the Freedmen's Bureau*, reflected this premise. Except for the earlier but ignored writing of W. E. B. DuBois in *The Souls of Black Folk* (1903), scholars did not begin to question the traditional view of the bureau until the 1950s. Since that time the historical emphasis has been on the bureau's accomplishments and its potential for social revolution. Ironically, the same white resistance that had been the key to the older view reappeared in the revisionist version, but this time as a major cause of the bureau's failure to be the instrument of social revolution that recent historians have said it might have been.

In retrospect, the Freedmen's Bureau could have become, with public and government support, one of the most effective instruments for the extension of human rights in American history. But white America was not yet ready for that, and the bureau fell far short of its potential. To begin with, it was very underfinanced. Although the Congress appropriated funds for buildings and other facilities, most of the teachers and medical workers were supported by private philanthropic groups. Not only did white Americans acquiesce in—and sometimes vigorously support—the southern objections to the bureau, but the conduct and attitude of the men entrusted with its administration undermined its effectiveness. In his recent biography, *Yankee Stepfather: General O. O. Howard and the Freedmen* (1968), William S. McFeely has pointed out that General Howard himself often "served to preclude rather than protect Negro freedom." In removing subordinates charged with corruption, Howard was often guided by the complaints of influential southern whites that these officials had been doing too much to help the freedmen. In other words, it appears that the white South could have lived with a corrupt bureau, but it could not live with a humanitarian one.

The Freedmen's Bureau was also to be the issue in the first

direct clash between the new president, Andrew Johnson, and the Republican-controlled Congress. When Johnson came to office in April 1865, the reactions of congressional leaders ranged from delight on the part of the Democrats to cautious acceptance by the Republicans. For the Democrats it meant that one of their own was in the White House. Johnson had been elected to the vice-presidency on the Union ticket in 1864, but that action had been dictated primarily by the exigencies of wartime. The substitution of the Union for the Republican label had been a ploy to win support of loyal Democrats and to cast an onus of antiunionism on the opposition candidate. But Johnson had never left the Democratic party; thus he could command the allegiance of almost all members, the old Copperheads who had opposed the northern war effort as well as those Democrats who had supported the war. Throughout April and May, Johnson was inundated with both pledges of support and thinly veiled appeals for patronage. "From all directions came the expectation of party reorganization," LaWanda and John H. Cox reported in *Politics, Principles, and Prejudice, 1865–1866: Dilemma of Reconstruction America* (1963), "with a powerful new coalition finding its center and leadership in Johnson himself."

At the same time, the radical Republicans, though disturbed by the president's preference for decentralized reconstruction and a minimum of federal interference, were pleased by the expectation that he would be easier to "handle" than Lincoln would have been. Johnson had always been a critic of the planter aristocracy and his initial public statements upon his succession to the presidency showed no change. Moreover, he had turned his back on his home state during the secession crisis and had gone with the Union. What greater tribute to a cause could a man pay? While this might have been seen by some as an example of iron will—even obstinacy—the Republicans preferred to see it as an example of political compatibility. Johnson had been vice-president for only a little more than a month, but his tenure as military governor of Tennessee, where he manipulated elections, imposed "iron-clad" oaths, and generally ruled with a dictatorial hand, was reassuring to most

Republican congressmen, especially after he announced that he would be guided by "those principles which governed me heretofore."

When the Congress adjourned in the spring of 1865, its radical members hoped that the president would repudiate the existing reconstructed state governments in the South and call the new Congress into special session instead of waiting for it to meet in regular session in December. Johnson began to discourage this hope when he announced on May 29 a Proclamation of Amnesty in which he extended forgiveness to all former Confederate officials, with full civil benefits, except for certain high-ranking and wealthy persons. But there was a loophole. The proclamation also allowed for the granting of "special" pardons to those not eligible for general amnesty, and in the subsequent months much of the president's time was taken up approving appeals for special pardons. The trouble was, in the minds of many Northerners, that he went too far. By granting what appeared to be wholesale pardons to former rebel leaders, Johnson, before long, had alienated a large part of his Republican and public support. Within three years he would be impeached.

It did not take long for southern whites to take advantage of what must have seemed to them an unexpected show of presidential sympathy. In the summer and fall of 1865, southern state legislatures instituted the notorious black codes. In some states the codes were merely updated versions of earlier laws applying to free blacks, with a few embellishments from the old slave codes thrown in. Whatever their origins, they amounted to a severe restriction of the civil rights of the former slaves. Some codes required blacks to have visible means of support. Mississippi's controversial vagrancy law allowed sheriffs to hire out any black arrested for vagrancy who could not pay his fine. Freedmen could not buy certain kinds of property; and the possession and acquisition of firearms and liquor were strictly controlled. Blacks were denied virtually all political rights, and in most states they could not testify in court. To white Southerners, emancipation did not mean equality. Although whites could no longer own blacks as property, the states retained the right to define the status of the freedmen. It did not take long for most Northerners to see that the southern states, given a free hand by an obsequious president, would reduce the freedmen to a level scarcely removed from slavery. It began to appear to the rest of the nation that the South had not learned its lesson in military defeat and would be incorrigible to the end.

Although the circumstances warranted the calling of a special session of the Congress, it was Johnson's intention to present it with a *fait accompli*. Accordingly, he took advantage of the long congressional summer and fall recess and directed the reconstruction of the seceded states more or less in accordance with Lincoln's plan (without the 10 percent provision), but incorporating a few features of the Wade-Davis bill. As he had less than seven months to accomplish this without congressional interference, speed was the most critical factor. Accordingly, whites in each southern state moved quickly. By December, every former Confederate state except Texas had reorganized its government and had elected congressmen who awaited their seats in the forthcoming Thirty-Ninth Congress.

Yet there was a lingering ambiguity to all that was happening. Johnson could not check the Congress completely, and it was widely known that the Republicans would demand some part in the reconstruction process. Thus, as December approached, Americans in both political parties anxiously awaited the president's annual message for a clarification of his policy.

When the message finally came on December 6, the result was further confusion. True, the words themselves were clear enough and the message was forthright in some of its generalities, but its substance left many questions unanswered. Although Johnson stipulated that the freedmen must be protected in their political and economic rights, for example, he did not specify what those rights were or how they were to be guaranteed. Depending on how one read the message, the authority could be claimed by the president, the Congress, or the state and local governments. And no provision was made for black suffrage, a matter that many radical Republicans considered imperative. With each political faction interpreting the message to suit itself, the president could easily be accused of deliberate equivocation. There were extreme opinions across the country on how reconstruction should proceed, and Johnson was the man in the middle. By appearing to offer a little something to everyone, but not really offering much of anything to anyone, he hoped to offend no one.

Any doubts as to whether or not there would be a conflict between the president and the Congress were removed by the decision of the House of Representatives not to seat the southern members-elect at the opening session on December 4. Although this action preceded the president's annual message, the text of the message had been known for several days because advance copies had been sent to outlying newspapers. Moreover, the issue of seating southern representatives had been raised as early as March 1863, when the then Clerk of the House, Emerson Ethridge, had been directed to list on the roll only those members who had been elected in accordance with federal law or the laws of their states. As LaWanda and John Cox explain in considerable detail, a number of leading northern newspapers debated throughout the summer and fall of 1865 whether or not Congress was in fact required to list the names of the southern members-elect. When, by prearrangement, Clerk of the House Edward McPherson announced that he would not list their names because he would be usurping the House's prerogative to decide these matters for itself, the eventual outcome was determined. Controlled by the Republican party, the House of Representatives simply denied admission to the southern representatives elected under the Johnson reconstruction program. Although this was not an open act of defiance of the president, it appeared that way to many, including Andrew Johnson.

Still, the actions of the Congress in its first few weeks were not openly hostile toward the president, and members of both parties continued to hope that some kind of compromise could be achieved. In the same session in which the House denied the southern members their seats, Thaddeus Stevens moved to create a joint committee on reconstruction, composed of nine representatives and six senators. Patterned after the Committee on the Conduct of the War that had been set up in 1861 because of congressional dissatisfaction with the way the war was progressing, its mission was to review the status of the former Confederate states and report to the Congress. More significantly, it was a clear declaration by the Congress that it was going to have a hand in reconstruction, the president's wishes notwithstanding.

As with so many other matters, the historical view of the Joint Committee on Reconstruction has been modified by revisionist research. One of the staunchest critics of the radical Republicans, Claude G. Bowers, in his *The Tragic Era: The Revolution after Lincoln* (1929), portrayed the committee as a collection of extremists by comparing it to the Committee of Public Safety of the French Revolution. To be sure, Democrats and other critics of the radical Republicans often referred to Stevens, Sumner, and some of the others as "Jacobins." A more recent book, E. Merton Coulter's *The South during Reconstruction, 1865–1877* (1947), contends that the main purpose of the committee was to "discredit the Johnson [reconstruction] governments." But recent scholarship has shown that there was a lingering inclination among many congressmen not to force the issue; and when the committee's membership was finally announced, several leading radicals were excluded, most notably Senator Sumner of Massachusetts. As Eric McKitrick pointed out in *Andrew Johnson and Reconstruction* (1960), "its balance of power was noticeably on the moderate side."

It is significant that the decisive break between the president and the Congress came not over a radical action, but over one initiated by a moderate Republican. Following a holiday recess, Senator Lyman Trumbull of Illinois introduced two bills that led to the ultimate showdown. The first was a measure calling for the indefinite extension of the Freedmen's Bureau and an enlargement of some of its duties. The second was a civil rights bill and was largely a reaction to the black codes that had been passed by the freewheeling southern legislatures. By conferring citizenship on everyone born in the United States, the latter bill was designed to assure "all persons in the United States in their civil rights, and furnish the means of their vindication." To avoid later misunderstanding, Trumbull had cleared both bills with the president before he introduced them, and afterwards he received additional assurances that Johnson would not oppose either one. On February 6, 1866, the House of Representatives approved the Freedmen's Bureau bill by a substantial majority, winning even the votes of a number of Johnson supporters. On February 19, President Johnson vetoed the bill.

It was not so much the veto that shocked the Republicans, as the message that accompanied it. Since the Freedmen's Bureau was an agency of the War Department, the current bill was, Johnson argued, an unconstitutional extension of military power in peacetime. He further asserted that there was no lawful provision for federal "support of indigent persons," and that the bill would result in land being confiscated from its rightful owners, keep whites apprehensive and blacks restless, and create a self-perpetuating patronage monster. Unperturbed by the severity of the black codes, Johnson contended that the settlement of the status of the freedmen was a state and local problem. Such a view was a logical extension of the antebellum conservative belief that slavery was a domestic institution defined exclusively by the state. He further indicated his displeasure over the refusal to seat southern congressmen elected under his reconstruction program, and he pointed out that these members, as they were the ones directly affected, should have had the opportunity to debate and vote on the bill. With something of a slap on the wrist, he argued that, although the Congress had the right to establish rules for seating its own membership, it could not willfully deny or evict a state's constitutionally guaranteed representation. Hurling what a number of radicals took as a final insult, Johnson concluded that in the matter of reconstruction, the office of the president was the ultimate authority, and that as far as he was concerned, the seceded states had been fully restored. The gauntlet had been thrown down.

Although the Freedmen's Bureau bill was a reasonable measure and had the support of a number of congressional conservatives, and although the public outcry over the veto message was considerable, the Congress, with five Republicans who had voted to pass it now voting to sustain the president, was unable to override the veto. Nevertheless, the consequences of Johnson's action were swift and ominous. The day after the veto an angry Joint Committee on Reconstruction met and unanimously voted to submit a resolution stating that no senator or representative from a seceded state shall be seated until "Congress shall have declared such state entitled to representation." At the same time, Trumbull made a long speech defending his bill and indicating his dismay over what he considered the president's betrayal.

Herein lay the key to the tragedy of Andrew Johnson. His failure as president was a direct result of his loss of the moderate Republican support he had enjoyed up to this point. Johnson simply was unable to see how badly he needed this support, and he proceeded to undercut his congressional friends. Many people, in the Congress and out, had opposed the hard line of the radicals. But Johnson's intransigence pushed their patience to the point of exasperation and they reluctantly cast their lot with the advocates of "complete and thorough" reconstruction. When, three days after the veto, he allowed some hecklers to goad him into the foolish assertion that Stevens and Sumner were traitors and might have had a hand in Lincoln's assassination, the president virtually cut himself off from the Congress. If there were a radical conspiracy against him, as he had intimated when he read his veto message to the cabinet, he had played right into its hands.

The civil rights bill had better luck than the Freedmen's Bureau bill, and because it was to become the archetype for the Fourteenth Amendment, its provisions were also more far-reaching. For the first time, American citizenship was defined by federal law, and the government's right to intervene in the protection of a citizen's civil rights was specifically asserted. Persons defined as citizens had the right to sue, testify in court, acquire and sell property, and enjoy the "full and equal benefit of all laws" without regard to race or color. A fundamental element of the proposal was the contention that the national government could compel a state to grant its citizens equal protection of the state's laws. With Northerners growing impatient toward what they considered an unrepentent South, Trumbull had clearly aimed the bill at the southern state governments. Violators were subject to arrest and fine or imprisonment by federal authorities, and the army and navy could be called upon to assist the enforcement. The civil rights bill was not punitive or extreme, and it won the support of all but three Republican senators. Moreover, the northern public response was overwhelmingly in favor of it. But President Johnson, spurning the near-unanimous advice of his cabinet, vetoed the bill, arguing that it was an unwarranted infringement on states' rights.

Thoroughly disgusted with the president's refusal to approve even the most moderate congressional measures, the few hesitant Republicans who had remained loyal to Johnson joined, on April 9, 1866 (the first anniversary of the surrender at Appomattox), in overriding the veto. Emboldened by their success, Republicans in the Congress rammed through a third Freedmen's Bureau bill and easily overrode another veto. The point of no return had been passed. With the knowledge that they could now enact any legislation they wanted to, regardless of the president, the Republicans in Congress launched their reconstruction program. Except for the second Freedmen's Bureau bill, every important reconstruction measure passed by the Congress during the remainder of Johnson's term was enacted into law, usually over his veto. Andrew Johnson has the dubious distinction of being the most overridden president in American history.

EQUAL PROTECTION OF THE LAWS

It is interesting to speculate on how the exacting and uncompromising military governor of Tennessee became the leading defender of white racism and southern states' rights. "No change of attitude and policy was ever more startling," the Coxes wrote, "than Johnson's transformation from an advocate of vengeance . . . to the embodiment of Executive clemency." Probably the most important reason for the change was the simple fact that the entire South was not Tennessee. Matters were much less complicated when dealing with just one state, and Johnson's tenure in Tennessee had been in wartime when a martial posture was easier to justify. The problems he had faced as a governor were simple compared to the enormity of his new responsibility. For example, in Tennessee Johnson had not faced the racial issue. He could rule with an iron fist and play one class of whites off against another and still uphold white supremacy. When civil rights for blacks entered the picture, it became an entirely different situation. Moreover, Johnson's vindictiveness towards the planter class altered drastically following the collapse of the Confederacy, while the entreaties from those around him in his initial weeks as president appealed to his vanity and to a weakness for patronizing. To be sure, there seems to be a contradiction between Johnson's past reputation for inflexibility and the ease with which he switched sides. But it is also true that he did not change as much as most historians have believed. Andrew Johnson was an independent thinker. "To an almost abnormal degree," McKitrick wrote, "he was a man who made up his own mind." The trouble was, when he began to suspect that he was a target of a conspiracy, that independence of mind became an almost paranoid obstinacy.

The role of party politics was also an important factor in Johnson's conduct. As military governor and vice-president, he was committed to the policies of the Republican administration. But it would have been politically illogical for a Democratic president to continue behaving like a Republican when the need for wartime unity no longer existed. With Lincoln's assassination, Johnson was suddenly thrust into the Democratic leadership, and he had an obligation to his party, through both the patronage and the exercise of his duties, to align himself in contrast to the opposition. Throughout the war the Democratic party had remained conservative on the issue of reconstruction. The Coxes contend that Johnson assumed he would become the guiding force in a new political alignment of Democrats and conservative Republicans. If this was the case, his alienation of the moderate Republicans was a strange way of achieving that end.

Meanwhile, the Joint Committee on Reconstruction concluded its investigation and in its report, which was largely the work of Stevens, William Pitt Fessenden, John A. Bingham, George Boutwell, and Roscoe Conkling, recommended a proposal that was to become the Fourteenth Amendment. The importance of this measure is difficult to exaggerate. In the words of British historian W. R. Brock, author of *An American Crisis: Congress and Reconstruction, 1865–1867* (1963), it "effected a fundamental alteration in the character of the Constitution . . . which could have been enacted at no other time." To modern civil libertarians the Fourteenth Amendment is the warp and woof of individual freedom in the United States. It is true that in the decades following reconstruction, it was more often invoked against the interests of the common man, as corporations hid under its protection to escape the restrictions of state antitrust regulation. In its first forty-three years, the amendment was the basis of 604 cases to come before the Supreme Court, of which only 28 involved black Americans, and with only 6 of these decided in the blacks' favor.

This use—or misuse—of the amendment does not, however, diminish its intrinsic worth. The first section defined citizenship and guaranteed to every *person* "due process" and "equal protection of the laws," *as each state defines its laws.* This was the heart of the Fourteenth Amendment. As worded, it prohibited a state from discriminating on the basis of race, although, as Joseph B. James reminded us in *The Framing of the Fourteenth Amendment* (1956), there were many people, including some of its supporters, who did not interpret it so broadly. The second section was more politically motivated. For a long time, as we have seen, Republicans had feared that the reconstructed southern states would send only conservatives to Washington. With their increased membership in the House of Representatives due to the elimination of the three-fifths provision, these new legislators could combine with the northern Democrats to overturn everything that had been accomplished. Northern business and financial interests also feared that southern congressmen would work to reverse or alter the new banking laws and protective tariffs that had been passed during the war. The Freedmen's Bureau and the Civil Rights Act of 1866, radicals feared, were in danger; and other measures, pending and planned, would never materialize. Since the framers of the amendment were also convinced that southern whites would do everything they could to keep the freedmen from voting, this section provided that whenever a state denied or abridged the suffrage right "in any way," that state's representation in the House would be reduced accordingly.

The third section of the Fourteenth Amendment removed from public life those ex-Confederates who had held federal or state office prior to secession. Their defection to engage in "insurrection or rebellion" or to give "aid and comfort to the enemies" of the United States was a violation of their oath to uphold the Constitution and, in the minds of some radical Republicans, was tantamount to treason. While the intent of this section was clearly to punish, there was also a provision permitting Congress to waive the disability.

In June the Congress passed the Fourteenth Amendment and sent it to the states for ratification. Although the president had no official duty, he took the occasion to criticize the measure and argue that no constitutional amendment should be proposed until the southern representation to the Congress had been seated and could participate in the deliberations. Tennessee, already under the control of the unionist government of William G. "Parson" Brownlow, ratified the amendment and was fully restored to the Union with an enabling act that

Johnson reluctantly signed. Otherwise, the Congress was having trouble getting much accomplished. A proposal to grant suffrage to the blacks of Washington, D.C., had been languishing in committee since December 1865, as the legislators seemed somewhat less enthusiastic about impartial suffrage when it got close to their office doors. The bill finally reached the president's desk where, on January 7, 1867, he vetoed it. The very next day, while Johnson was luxuriating in the praise of Democratic newspaper editorials, both houses of Congress overrode the veto. The Congress also debated other matters but made virtually no progress. The big question—What, if anything, were the Republicans going to demand of the seceded states as a condition for full restoration?—remained unanswered. For the rest of 1866, no major reconstruction legislation was passed, and many people began to assume that all a seceded state had to do was follow Tennessee's example.

Even if the ratification of the Fourteenth Amendment had been all that was required for full restoration, it would have taken more to get the white South to agree than the persuasion of its moderate friends. Inspired partly by the president's outspoken opposition to the amendment, all ten of the other former Confederate states, plus Delaware and Kentucky, refused to ratify. This meant that the necessary three-fourths could not be realized unless at least three of these states changed their minds. And although Tennessee had already set a precedent, there was still some uncertainty about the legitimacy of an unrestored state's ratification. The Congress had, after all, challenged the legality of the state governments and had put them on notice that they would have to meet certain conditions before they could resume full statehood. Until such time, the states remained in an undefined limbo under the eye of the army. But if the seceded states were not fully recognized, how could ratification of an amendment be demanded of them? The Constitution stipulates that only states can ratify an amendment. If Alabama was not recognized by the national government as a state, it had no legal right to ratify an amendment and the Congress could not require it to do so. On the other hand, if the rebel states did not legally qualify as states, should they count as part of the total states? Apparently. The ratification of the Thirteenth Amendment had followed the adoption of a rule by the Department of State, which certified ratifications, that all states should be counted regardless of their unreconstructed status. Later, however, Texas's ratification of the Fifteenth Amendment was not counted in the total until that state was formally readmitted in March 1870.

It would be easy, in the light of all this, to criticize the radicals for being opportunists, but that is a temptation one should resist. The political party that did not exploit its advantages was not a very effective party. Beyond that was a simple matter of the need for adjustment. The Republicans may have been guilty of contradiction, inconsistency, or even hypocrisy, but at least their feet were not stuck in cement. With the passage of time it became necessary to adjust to changing conditions. At the beginning of the war probably not even the abolitionists anticipated reconstruction as an opportunity to remake the fabric of American society. But few wars have ended on the note they began on; by 1865 things had changed drastically, including the political temper of many Americans. If complete and thorough reconstruction made political sense in 1865, why should critics discredit it simply because it had not been the prevailing view in 1861?

It is inherent in the American constitutional system that whenever the president and the Congress engage in a struggle for supremacy, chaos can be the result. The separation of powers is a mixed blessing. Conceived to preclude arbitrary and precipitous conduct on the part of one branch of the government, this three-headed creature (four-headed when the two houses of Congress are at odds) has also prevented the government from acting decisively. As a European observer of the American scene put it: "what was at stake in reconstruction was . . . the ability of a government of separate powers to deal with a crisis," a condition that Alexis de Tocqueville had criticized three decades before the Civil War. Moreover, while the mere existence of separate powers was troublesome enough, it was even worse if there were basic philosophical differences among them. In such times, progressive change—or what one branch saw as progressive change—was hard to achieve. That the Congress was able to do what it did during the reconstruction—and that was considerable—was, among other things, a tribute to its ability to overcome constitutional limitations. Historians are fond of pointing out that the greatest presidents in American history have usually been men who were not afraid to bend the Constitution now and then, i.e., to check and unbalance checks and balances. In the years following the Civil War the Congress was the big Constitution bender. Yet one should be cautious in praising the radical Republicans. Despite their successes in advancing the cause of human rights, they still did not achieve many of their goals. Moreover, speculation over the damage they might have done had they not been checked occasionally, and a review of the excesses that seemed to characterize political life everywhere in the country, remind us that the conflict in a system of separate powers is a small price to pay for its virtues.

In the last analysis, the question of responsibility was moot. Even before Lincoln's assassination, the radicals in the Congress were determined to assert themselves. Lincoln's pocket-veto of the Wade-Davis bill indicated that he was opposed to a hard line, but he would not have been able to pocket-veto his way through reconstruction. With Andrew Johnson in the White House an executive-legislative conflict was more certain because the inflexible Tennesseean created opportunities for the radicals that Lincoln would never have given them. Moreover, Lincoln's high reputation at the end of the war gave him more political clout than Johnson ever enjoyed, an advantage he would have exploited fully. But it should not be forgotten that the radicals did not have an easy time overcoming Johnson's resistance. His veto of the second Freedmen's Bureau bill was sustained; and it was not until after the congressional elections of 1866, when northern voters expressed their resentment toward his leniency in dealing with former rebels, that the radicals gained the upper hand. Until then, there were enough conservatives in the

Republican party who, combined with the Democrats, allowed the president to keep the initiative. By his action, Johnson gave the Congress much of the ammunition that it used to overcome him. Abraham Lincoln would not have been so clumsy.

There has also been a good deal of speculation that had Lincoln lived, his goodwill and political common sense would have moderated the radical demands, resulting in a more charitable and generous (to whites) reconstruction. In his introduction to the 1967 edition of William B. Hesseltine's *Lincoln's Plan of Reconstruction* (originally published in 1960), Richard N. Current noted that this belief has been especially popular in the South. (Exalting Lincoln makes the radicals look worse.) The belief is based partly on the assumption that Lincoln would have been more sympathetic with the proposals of moderate Republicans and would continue to enjoy their support. With the concluding sentence of Lincoln's Second Inaugural Address still ringing in their ears, Americans who held this view saw the death of Lincoln as an omen of evil times. Somehow, he would have made everything all right.

But such a conciliatory view also supposes that Lincoln would not have pressed the South to accept the Fourteenth Amendment. Such a supposition is hard to accept. If Lincoln was as magnanimous as he has been made out to be by those who point to his charity, he could not have objected to something as patently libertarian as the Fourteenth Amendment. He had indicated his support for the proposed Thirteenth Amendment, so he evidently had not objected to the use of the Constitution for moral reform. In view of the situation that existed in 1866–1867, the Fourteenth Amendment was a logical extension of that idea. Conversely, Lincoln could not have made reconstruction less troublesome by persuading the ten southern states to follow Tennessee's example and ratify the amendment. Anyone familiar with the nature of the white South in the nineteenth century must concede that this would have been impossible. As Michael Perman has pointed out in *Reunion Without Compromise: The South and Reconstruction: 1865–1868*

(1973), Southerners were unwilling to accept any kind of reconstruction, presidential or congressional.

THE RECONSTRUCTION ACTS

With the black codes receiving daily press coverage in the North, with the stubbornness of the president becoming a national embarrassment, and with the white Southerners growing more defiant, northern public opinion moved steadily toward "complete and thorough" reconstruction. The refusal of all but one of the former Confederate states to ratify the Fourteenth Amendment was viewed by many Northerners as the extreme act of southern incorrigibility. In looking back, the amendment, like the Civil Rights Act of 1866, does not appear to have been oppressive or unreasonable. Whatever southern leaders thought they had to gain by refusing to ratify it is difficult to perceive. In approving it they would have lost little and, if they were not too offensive about it, they could have retained control of their state and local governments. But the essence of the amendment was so diametrically opposed to everything the white Southerner believed in that he simply could not "bite the bullet" and accept it. He had lost the war, suffered tremendous property destruction, and seen over two billion dollars' worth of slaves evaporate. He was in no mood to be agreeable, let alone contrite. Thus by his attitude and actions he brought down upon his back the wrath of the radicals in Congress. The unreconstructed white Southerner, as much as anybody, was responsible for his own misery.

On March 2, 1867, almost two years after the end of the war, Congress passed the first Reconstruction Act. Under its terms, the former Confederate states (Tennessee was excluded) were divided into five military districts, each headed by a general who was the supreme authority within the district. Only the First District was comprised of just one state, Virginia. The existing civil governments, meaning those organized under the Johnson program, were allowed to continue on a provisional basis, subordinate to the district authority. The bill ordered the military commander to call for the election of delegates to a constitutional convention in each state, provided that blacks must be allowed to vote and that whites disqualified by the Fourteenth Amendment (which had not yet been ratified) be disfranchised. Moreover, the law specified that both of these suffrage provisions be written into each new state constitution, which must then be approved by a majority of the qualified voters. After all these steps had been taken and its legislature had ratified the Fourteenth Amendment, a seceded state could then send representatives to Congress and it would be considered fully restored.

The bill ran into two immediate obstacles. The first was the president's veto. Though Johnson was outraged at the Congress's claim of exclusive responsibility, his veto message was relatively restrained. In it he said that the Reconstruction Act was "without precedent and without authority, in palpable conflict with the plainest provisions of the Constitution, and utterly destructive to those great principles" for which so many Americans had died in earlier wars. Virtually all of the actions called for in the act, he argued, were state prerogatives. In short, there was simply no constitutional authority for the Congress's demands. Moreover, by not only dictating that blacks should vote but how they should vote, the federal government was launching a plan that would lead to "Africanizing the southern part of our territory." But by now practically no one was listening to Andrew Johnson. The Congress quickly passed the first Reconstruction Act over his veto.

The second obstacle was confusion, and it took longer to overcome. The Reconstruction Act left many things unsaid. For example, there were no explicit instructions on how the registration and election process in each state should be initiated. With the law calling for the continuation of existing governments until the new ones were set up, the people of a state could, conceivably, choose to remain under their current system by doing nothing, as indeed some of them tried to do. To get the program off dead center, therefore, the Congress, in the second

Reconstruction Act of March 23, directed the military commanders to take the initiative, spelled out the procedures for registrations and elections, and drew up an "iron-clad" oath. On July 19, yet another act was passed over the president's veto that enabled registration boards to deny registration to anyone they thought had not taken the oath in good faith, a provision that invited abuse because a board could disfranchise someone with only a tissue of evidence. The law also set forth a number of explanatory statements on the "true intent and meaning" of all the reconstruction acts.

The Congress then sat back to see how these laws worked out, but there were still problems. When it was discovered in Alabama that whites could undermine the intent of the referendum requirement by registering and not voting, the Congress, on March 11, 1868, passed a fourth Reconstruction Act that required a majority of only the votes cast for approval of a new constitution. This final act, which became law under the ten-day rule instead of a veto override, also simplified voter eligibility by requiring only ten days' residence in an election district, a provision designed for the freedmen, many of whom were wandering around trying to get relocated. Thus was the machinery of congressional reconstruction established.

Although the Congress had taken the initiative from the president, it had not forgotten him. Some Republicans feared that Johnson would try to overturn congressional reconstruction, especially after he said that he might take certain actions in the South "regardless of the consequences." On the same day the first Reconstruction Act was passed, Congress passed two other laws designed not only to remove the president from the reconstruction picture, but to remove him altogether. In a rider to an army appropriations act, Congress limited his authority as commander-in-chief by requiring him to issue all military orders through the so-called General of the Army, who happened to be Ulysses S. Grant. The second measure was the Tenure-of-Office Act, which took the Senate's constitutional duty of confirmation and turned it around. It specified that a civil officer whose appointment had required senatorial approval could not be removed until a successor was named who had also been approved by the Senate. In effect, it made the procedure for removal of such an official the same as the procedure for his appointment, which meant that the president could not dismiss a cabinet member without the Senate's approval. While one of the purposes of the act was, as revisionist historian Kenneth M. Stampp, in *The Era of Reconstruction, 1865–1877* (1965), pointed out, "to prevent Johnson from using his patronage power against the Republicans as he had done in the congressional elections of 1866," it was obvious that there was more to it than that. The Tenure-of-Office Act explicitly made a violation of its terms a "high misdemeanor," which is what it would take to impeach the president. Andrew Johnson was being set up.

Even so, it was not easy. For over a year prior to February 1868, when a committee was established in the House of Representatives to draw up impeachment articles, the radicals had made a number of unsuccessful attempts to bring formal charges against the president. It was not until Johnson tried to remove Secretary of War Edwin M. Stanton that the Congress succeeded in bringing its case to trial. The president named three different men to replace Stanton, but none was confirmed by the Senate, and the secretary barricaded himself in his office. On February 24, before it had even decided on specific charges, the House voted 126 to 47 to impeach Johnson for "high crimes and misdemeanors in office." Following a vituperative speech by Thaddeus Stevens that he was too ill to finish himself, the *ad hoc* committee listed eleven charges against Johnson, eight of them based on his attempt to remove Stanton, one related to the Command-of-the-Army Act, and two pertaining to his speeches and overall conduct. On March 2 and 3, the House adopted all eleven articles.

The presiding judge of the trial in the Senate was Chief Justice Salmon P. Chase, a Republican. Benjamin F. Butler of Massachusetts launched the prosecution's case, but in the process he dwelt at length, and with increasingly intemperate language, not on any specific crime the president had allegedly committed, but on criticisms of the Congress that Johnson had made in public speeches. Butler was the author of Impeachment Article 10, which accused the president of "inflammatory, and scandalous harangues" against the Congress. In thus arguing their case, the Republican managers raised some dubious points. The proceedings were political, they admitted, not judicial; therefore it was not necessary to prove a crime in the orthodox sense. Such an assumption, of course, raised doubts as to the prosecution's motives. Resorting to shabby theatrics, Butler waved in the air a bloodstained shirt he claimed had belonged to an Ohio carpetbagger who had been beaten by whites in Mississippi. Thus was born the propaganda device that has ever since been called by historians "waving the bloody shirt."

Johnson himself was spared the humiliation of being present, and his defense presented a persuasive case. The president's attempt to test a law in court was not a crime, his lawyers argued, and that even if the Tenure-of-Office Act was upheld, it only applied to the president who had made the appointment in the first place. Lincoln, not Johnson, had named Stanton. When the first vote came on May 16, seven Republicans voted with the Democrats for a minority vote of 19 to 35—one short of the number needed for conviction. After ten days of Republican behind-the-scenes arm-twisting, two more votes were taken, but the results were the same and the radicals gave up. The trial was over.

An intriguing question to ponder is how it could have happened at all. The answer probably lay in the uniqueness of the situation. It was the combination of unusual circumstances, each one itself a major issue of public concern, that made the removal from office of a president of the United States a distinct possibility: (1) The nation was in the midst of an emotional upheaval following a bloody civil war; (2) a president had been murdered and succeeded by a man who had none of his predecessor's skill for handling critics; (3) a large portion of the country was devastated and torn with uncertainty and racism; and (4) the Congress was in the control of men who opposed the president bitterly and who themselves were both promoters and victims of the highly charged passions of the hour. The vengeful posture of the radical Republicans reflected a mood that, fortunately, is rarely visited on the American political scene. Their contempt for Johnson was so obsessive that public sympathy for the president, coming even from Republican sources, appeared before the trial actually began.

In the final analysis, Johnson's enemies in Congress, cocksure in their power, overplayed their hand. Persuading the members of the Senate to convict the president of a crime is a lot different from persuading them to override a veto. But the fact that the radicals almost succeeded is a chilling reminder that not even the American system of checks and balances is foolproof. The fact that they failed is a reassuring reminder that the system can endure extreme challenges.

GUARANTEEING ASCENDANCY

The most controversial, and certainly the most emotion-charged aspect of congressional reconstruction was the provision calling for black suffrage. Despite the profound moral tone that climaxed the Civil War, the United States was a racist nation. For decades, white Americans had boasted of their humble origins and their devotion to democracy and the common man; but they never meant to include Negroes, Indians, Asians, or other nonwhite peoples in the American Dream. Giving political rights to thousands of illiterate and propertyless ex-slaves who, many whites believed, were scarcely removed from an ancestry of cannibalism and other barbaric practices, was totally inconceivable. Incapable of civilized behavior, black voters would, whites insisted, corrupt the political process by selling their votes to the highest bidder. Where blacks were in the majority, their primitive instincts would overpower and utterly destroy democratic society, as many whites believed had happened in Haiti. The whole idea was fraught with evil, conservatives complained, and was the most terrible of the many iniquities of radical reconstruction.

To prove their argument, critics pointed out that in the North only the New England states (Connecticut excepted), where abolitionists were most fanatical and reckless—and where, conveniently, the black population was relatively small—permitted blacks to vote without discriminatory requirements. In most other northern states they were not allowed to vote at all, and in the several states where the issue had been put to the voters in the postwar years, it was almost always soundly defeated. By the time the Fifteenth Amendment was ratified in March 1870, half of the northern states—13 out of 26—still denied the ballot to blacks. How, then, could the members of the Congress whose own constituents were opposed to black suffrage justify forcing it on another section of the country, a section without a voice in the Congress and therefore unable even to participate in the decision? Obviously, the radical Republicans had left themselves wide open to charges of hypocrisy. It could even be argued that the Congress was using black suffrage to punish an unrepentant South, which, if true, was a tacit admission that black suffrage was repugnant.

The proponents answered these criticisms by arguing that the issue in the North was not the same as in the South where the freedmen had to have political power to protect themselves from their former oppressors. If southern blacks could not exercise power commensurate with their numbers, they would be helpless against the old planter oligarchy. Few Republicans disputed the principle of state and local sovereignty in elections where *all* eligible voters had an equal voice in selecting officeholders. As long as only white men voted, however, those elected would not represent the entire population. On the assumption that people voted primarily to advance their own interests, it could be expected that the two races in the South would support different candidates. At least that was the supposition, and it was a reasonable one. Impartial suffrage was, therefore, not merely a matter of granting certain persons the right to vote, but a matter of survival for almost 40 percent of the South's population. On the other hand, Republicans fatuously told critics, no such need for self-protection existed in the North. Northern blacks had always been free, and their small numbers would have little effect on the total vote anyway. The sections were just too different, radicals argued, for the rule to apply uniformly. The fact that the northern black faced universal discrimination and had little recourse seemed to elude them entirely.

Since southern whites would never voluntarily share civil rights with the freedmen, some kind of federal mandate was imperative. But it would be hard to imagine a more impossible place to establish racial harmony than the post–Civil War South. A vast black population, ignorant, propertyless, unevenly distributed, and one step removed from chattel slavery (and to whom most whites believed they owed nothing), was at one extreme; a small coterie of landed aristocrats, with a habit of social and political preeminence, was at the other; and a yeoman farmer but largely poor white population, which traditionally deferred to the gentry, occupied the great middle. On the side was a small minority engaged in commerce, finance, the trades, and the professions. With such a mix, the white South had what it considered to be the best answer: blacks must be totally excluded from social and political life, and confined to those activities for which they were peculiarly suited. Since the African race was so patently inferior and so obviously incapable of self-government, it was not only the best answer, it was the only answer.

From a practical standpoint, many Republicans believed that they needed the southern black vote for *their* survival. The Republican party was still a sectional party, and its success thus far was due in large measure to the fact that the Democratic party had lost a substantial portion of its national leadership and power when the South seceded. What would happen when the southern Democrats returned to full partnership with their northern colleagues? As noted earlier, the question of the Republican party's future and the restoration of the South had been an issue since the initial discussions of reconstruction during the war. Lincoln had hoped to win the support of the old southern Whig element by being magnanimous and sympathetic. The radicals, on the other hand, had committed themselves to a program in which the Republican party forced itself into a commanding position by virtue of the black vote and the reconstruction process. They were convinced that the vast majority of southern whites would be so embittered by the war that no amount of charity would conciliate any significant number of them. Accordingly, by the time the first Reconstruction Act was passed, the radicals were openly conceding that the vote of the freedmen was essential for "guaranteeing the ascendancy" of the Republican party.

Moreover, the complaint that most of the 700,000 eligible black voters in the South were too ignorant to vote intelligently, so long echoed by traditional historians, was specious. As John Hope Franklin reminded us in *Reconstruction: After the Civil War* (1961), "they were not unlike the large number of Americans who were enfranchised during the age of Jackson or the large number of immigrants who were being voted in herds by political bosses in New York, Boston, and other American cities at this time." Or, Franklin might have added, the even larger number of immigrants, many illiterate and unable to speak English, who would be organized by ward captains in the early twentieth century. Granting that southern blacks were poorly prepared to exercise independent political judgment, the defenders of black suffrage reminded the critics of the reasons for this sad state of affairs. The freedman had just come out of two centuries of chattel slavery, during which he had no rights and was prohibited from acquiring even the most rudimentary skills like reading and writing. If anything, the white South now had an obligation to rectify the situation by supporting every effort to improve his status.

There was also an economic aspect of guaranteeing Republican ascendancy. As noted earlier, manufacturing, commerce, and finance had benefited greatly by government borrowing and spending and the passage of favorable laws. The best way to encourage continued investment in free enterprise, Senator Charles Sumner admitted, was to ensure the predominance of the Republican party, which meant giving the ballot to the freedmen. Entrepreneurs believed that the southern leaders, once restored to their former positions of influence in the national government, would try to overturn all of the new laws. From the 1820s on, southern congressmen and presidents had opposed tariffs, central banking, and appropriations for internal improvements. Blessed with an extensive river system and committed to a monoculture that produced mainly for export, Southerners had tried, usually successfully, to defeat every proposal that seemed primarily in the interests of the Northeast and Midwest. Additionally, midwestern farmers had long resented the South's opposition to a more liberal public land policy. Northeastern and midwestern interests had their differences, W. R. Brock observed in his *An American Crisis: Congress and Reconstruction, 1865–1867* (1963), but both "had reason to regard the former policy of the South as having been, at some point, harmful and obstructive. The picture of the South as the enemy of economic progress completed the picture of the South as opposed to that government whose object was the betterment of mankind."

If the Republican party needed an object lesson in its dependence on black votes, the presidential election of 1868—a classic example of the efficiency of bloc voting—was perfect for the occasion. Not that the candidates themselves presented much of a contrast on the race issue. At the Republican convention in Chicago in May, the delegates nominated the "man of the hour," Ulysses S. Grant, on the first ballot. No one else was even considered, although several people had been mentioned in the preceding months. So attractive was Grant as a military hero that for a time the Democrats had even thought of nominating him.

In contrast, the Democrats, meeting in New York City in July, seemed as though they would never agree. There were at least a dozen men being mentioned, though some had only slim chances. Almost as if to exemplify the Democratic confusion, one of the preconvention favorites had been Chief Justice Salmon P. Chase, a Republican. With government fiscal policies contending with reconstruction as the chief campaign issue, the Democrats, on the twenty-second ballot, finally settled on the former governor of New York, Horatio Seymour. Saddled with a capable but colorless candidate running against a war hero, discredited by its extremist Copperhead faction, embarrassed by the conduct of its titular head, and burdened by the taint of disloyalty that followed from its association with the South, the Democratic party should have been the victim of a Republican landslide. Grant won, but the Republican party received one of the biggest frights of its life.

Grant defeated Seymour by an electoral vote of 214 to 80. But in the popular vote, he received just a little over 52 percent of the total: 3,013,421 to 2,706,829. The most shocking aspect, however, was not the closeness of the popular vote, but the distribution of the racial vote. Approximately a half million blacks went to the polls, most of them newly enfranchised freedmen; and all but about 50,000 of them cast their ballots for Grant. The Republican war hero was in fact the choice of a minority of the white voters of the United States. It is true that the distribution of the white votes probably would have given Grant an electoral majority anyway, so it is incorrect to assert that he was elected by blacks. But that did not diminish the significance of the racial vote. At the same time, it was becoming clear that political equality in the South was too fragile to survive solely on the strength of the reconstruction acts. And there was ample evidence that northern whites were as opposed to black suffrage as ever. The race question had been the most inflammatory issue of the campaign, with the Democratic candidates and other party speakers stumping throughout the North denouncing Republican "Africanization" policies. In the last analysis, white racism was a major factor in Seymour's strong showing. At the same time, the election results also illustrated that, as supporters of Negro suffrage had been saying all along, blacks did indeed need the ballot for their own protection—and not just in the South. Thus the noise of Republican victory celebrations had hardly died out when party leaders drafted the Fifteenth Amendment.

Although the debate over black suffrage—what William Gillette in his *The Right to Vote: Politics and the Passage of the Fifteenth Amendment* (1965) called the "Knot of Reconstruction"

—had gone on since 1864, it intensified dramatically in the months following the election of 1868. In January and February of 1869, the congressional debates over the proposed amendment were long and heated, and the discussion in the national press was no less animated. Finally, on February 26, the Senate approved a compromise and the resolution was sent to the state legislatures—where it met another round of challenges. (After elections in which Democrats regained control, the state legislatures of New York and Indiana voted to rescind their earlier ratifications.) It is true that the proposed amendment had a limited objective: enfranchising northern blacks and protecting southern blacks from disfranchisement. It is also true that it had been weakened considerably in the eyes of some Republicans who had wanted a guarantee of a black's right to hold office. Also, the amendment did not challenge the principle of state-defined voting qualifications, and it included no specific enforcement provisions. In short, it was not all it should have been.

But in reality, the supporters of black suffrage probably got the best that could be had. The Fifteenth Amendment was the work of the lame-duck Fortieth Congress. The attitude of many Republicans who would not be returning to the Capitol was that the suffrage amendment had to pass the Congress now because the newly elected Democrats (and Republicans) would surely kill it. If it is true that lame-duck congressmen have been guilty of recklessness and self-serving actions, it is also true that they have supported necessary and proper legislation that their previous dependence on a hostile constituency had discouraged. The Fifteenth Amendment was just such a measure.

CARPETBAGGERS AND SCALAWAGS

Up until recently, the popular image of the South during reconstruction was one of waste, turmoil, and corruption. The decade after the Civil War was a "Tragic Era." Republican charlatans, exploiting the opportunities to pillage and plunder, were overrunning the former Confederate states, Democrats and other white conservatives complained, and stealing the helpless citizens blind. Leading the rape of the prostrate South were the "carpetbaggers," northern adventurers who had been lured to the South by the chance to seize political office and who were interested only in personal profit and power. White Southerners universally characterized these interlopers as grasping, ignorant, unconscionable, filthy, and totally lacking in refinement or any other civilized quality. Eventually they applied the term to all outsiders: army officers, Freedmen's Bureau officials, teachers from northern colleges, relief workers from private and religious philanthropic organizations, and Republican organizers from the northern Union League clubs all bore the mark. Even today it is doubtful if there is a more reprehensible label in the southern politician's vocabulary than "carpetbagger," and the southern aversion to "outsiders" is still strong.

Allied with the carpetbaggers were the "scalawags," mostly poor white Southerners motivated not only by the chance for private gain, critics declared, but also by spite. Here was their chance to get even with the haughty plantation overlords who had been toppled by the war. If there was one thing that made the scalawags worse than the carpetbaggers, it was their treachery to their own states and section. At the bottom of the heap were the freedmen, given the vote by the new state constitutions and easily led by fast-talking demagogues. This was the melodrama of reconstruction. It was *The Birth of a Nation* (1915), a silent movie produced by the son of a Confederate officer. It was a continuation of *Uncle Tom's Cabin* with the roles of the Good Guys and Bad Guys reversed. And it was also bad history.

Richard N. Current, in his brief but provocative essay, "Carpetbaggers Reconsidered," *A Festschrift for Frederick B. Artz* (1964), pointed out that many of the best known carpetbaggers—Albion Tourgée, Willard Warner, and Albert T. and Charles Morgan, for example—had not gone south with the idea of seeking public office, but had migrated *before* the passage of the reconstruction acts and had risked their own capital in private ventures that would benefit the local economies. Eight of the nine carpetbaggers who eventually served as governors had also arrived in the South before 1867, and the ninth, Adelbert Ames of Maine and Mississippi, had been an army officer and military governor whose civil administration was scrupulously honest and fair. Of the sixty-two carpetbaggers who served in both houses of Congress, fifty had gone south before 1867, while half of the others had engaged in private business before getting involved in public affairs. A closer look at this group also turns up another surprise. White Southerners described carpetbaggers as "ignorant" or "of bad character," but Current revealed that of the sixty-two representatives and senators, forty-three had one or more years of college, most of them having practiced law, medicine, engineering, or teaching. In short, the majority of the "successful" carpetbaggers did not have unsavory backgrounds and "had moved South for reasons other than a lust for offices newly made available by the passage of the Reconstruction Acts."

Another misconception that historians too long allowed to endure was the length of carpetbagger rule. The reconstruction era is usually defined as the period from the end of the war in 1865 to 1877 when the last federal troops were removed from the South. Although no one has asserted that the carpetbaggers controlled the South for twelve years, the implication has lingered. The truth of the matter was that the carpetbaggers were in power in only parts of the South, and only there for short periods of time. Tennessee, never subjected to congressional reconstruction in the first place, returned to the control of white conservatives in 1869, and the other ten former Confederate states followed suit between 1870 and 1877. Even when a state remained in Republican control for more than a few months, it was just as often at the hands of southern unionists as of carpetbaggers. Over half of the southern states—six out of eleven—never had a carpetbagger governor; and of those carpetbaggers who became governors, few of them were in office very long, and they were supported by scalawags and freedmen. In fact, Harrison Reed of Florida, Current reminded us in another work, *Three Carpetbag Governors* (1967), "got himself elected largely by catering to conservative Southerners."

No state legislature had a carpetbagger majority, and where carpetbaggers did have substantial power, it was also based on southern unionist support, black and white. In his article "Carpetbagger Constitutional Reform in the South Atlantic States, 1867–1868," *Journal of Southern History* (1961), Jack B. Scroggs even suggested that the South might have been better off with more, not fewer, carpetbaggers. "The states with the most able carpetbagger leadership emerged with the most democratic and progressive constitutions," Scroggs asserted, "and, as able Northern leadership decreased, the liberality of the documents tended to decrease proportionally." There were individuals, more numerous in some places than in others, whose activities were not in the public interest, but the general portrait of the entire South victimized by a lot of unscrupulous soldiers of fortune from the North is largely a fiction.

While revisionist historians have done much to destroy the myth of the carpetbaggers, others have laid the groundwork for a fresh look at the scalawags. In his article "Who Were the Scalawags?" *Journal of Southern History* (1963), Allen Trelease took issue with certain revisionist historians who suggested that most of the scalawags were "old-line" Whigs who had opposed secession from the beginning. This was the case, he argued, in no more than three of the southern states. Basing his conclusions on a statistical analysis of the voting records of 843 southern counties, Trelease contended that the "great majority of native white Republicans . . . [were] hill country farmers" who more often than not had been Democrats, but were drawn to the Republican policy of government aid to economic developments. In other words, the attraction of the Republican party for the "plain folk" of the South was not based on a long-held resentment against the planter class, but on a favorable reaction to what was essentially a populist appeal to the small farmer.

There were, nonetheless, more than a few prominent Southerners in the scalawag camp. James A. Longstreet, a former Confederate general and one of Robert E. Lee's most competent field commanders; James L. Orr of South Carolina who had been a leader of the secession movement and represented his state in the Confederate Senate; and R. W. Flournoy, a wealthy Mississippi planter who had owned many slaves; all worked for the Republican cause and were severely condemned by their conservative neighbors. Vernon Lane Wharton pointed out in his highly acclaimed *The Negro in Mississippi, 1865–1890* (1947) that the "Republican leadership in Mississippi contained an unusually large number of prominent white men who were old residents of the state." The revisionist view of the scalawags is still unfolding, but enough is already known to indicate that the popular characterization of them as renegades was as great a canard as the traditional portrayal of the carpetbaggers as rogues.

Although the benefits of Republican reconstruction were uneven, a careful look at the South reveals a list of impressive accomplishments. All of the new state constitutions, despite numerous variations, were improvements over the old ones. The constitutional conventions reorganized the branches of government, set limitations on the use of public credit, established permanent relief measures protecting homesteads, created state-wide free public education systems, overhauled archaic judicial systems, liberalized qualifications for public officeholding, re-defined city and county powers, and updated voting and election codes so as to remove restrictions that had discriminated against the poor. In North Carolina a religious test for voting was abolished. Many of these changes were instituted specifically to break the power of the planters who had dominated southern life for so long. To the extent that the Republicans were successful, be they carpetbaggers or scalawags, the quality of life for all Southerners was improved.

Nor did the accomplishments end with the constitutions. Conservatives complained of excessive taxes, and taxes were higher than they had ever been before, but the South, with a history of opposition to taxes, had always had low revenue schedules. What seemed like excessive taxation was really necessary taxation, imposed by the Republicans to provide essential facilities and services that the Old South had never thought important. What conservatives often called "stealing" was money appropriated for schools, hospitals, sanitation facilities, transportation and communications developments, and public works, needs in which the South, because of its long-standing opposition to internal improvements and an indifference to the general welfare, lagged far behind the rest of the country. The Republican state governments also ratified the Fourteenth and Fifteenth Amendments, revised tax and real estate laws in favor of the poor, abolished imprisonment for debt, and curtailed cruel and unusual punishments like branding, whipping, and the stocks. These were indeed radical changes because they were so contrary to the status quo of the conservative white establishment in the South. Reconstruction was revolutionary, and revolution means upheaval. But the point that students of reconstruction should keep in mind is that these changes were largely beneficial and necessary. The popular view of them as arbitrary and capricious was promulgated by those who wanted no changes.

This does not mean that there was no corruption or bad government in the South. A nation, or state, struggling back from defeat in war passes through a state of extreme flux, and there are always opportunists who will exploit the turmoil for personal gain. But all of this should be viewed in the proper perspective. In the first place, Democrats and other white conservatives were also guilty of misconduct in office. The greatest corruption in Mississippi, for example, occurred before 1867 while the state was still under the Johnson program. Flagrant corruption among Republicans was conspicuous in only a few states, notably Florida, South Carolina, Alabama, and Louisiana. In the other seven former Confederate states, the amounts stolen from state treasuries were relatively insignificant. There were also opportunities for graft at the local levels, but, though the degree of corruption varied, the sums were usually small because most local governments were impoverished. Corrupt carpetbaggers, in Current's words, "were few and relatively unimportant."

It should also be remembered that the reconstruction era was the heyday of spoilsmen everywhere. It was the beginning of the Gilded Age. When viewed against the brazen activities of both Democratic and Republican politicians in other parts of the country, southern Republicans who used their offices for personal profit were amateurs. The South Carolina State Legislature appropriated $1,000 to reimburse the Speaker of the House for losses suffered in gambling and entertainment. But in New York City, William Marcy Tweed and his Tammany Hall associates cheated the taxpayers out of tens of millions of dollars, with some estimates placing the figure at 90 percent of the city's receipts. By granting charters, subsidies, loans, and public land in exchange for stock options and other favors, numerous members of the Congress found railroad legislation very profitable. Or, when they wanted to be more direct about it, they simply voted themselves a "salary grab" bonus of $5,000 each. Personal fortunes were also made by officials in the administration as "conflict of interest" was the order of the day. The Whiskey Ring, the Star Route frauds, and the Indian Bureau scandals involved persons who could be traced up to the office of the president. Compared to all this, the corruption in the South was trifling. Indeed, it is surprising that there was not more.

REGAINING THE "LOST CAUSE"

If what we were long led to believe about carpetbaggers and scalawags was so inaccurate and distorted, how did such a version get established in the first place, and why did it endure so long?

The answer rests, in large measure, in the primary sources that scholars consulted when studying the reconstruction period. Earlier historians compiled most of their evidence from southern documents, a procedure bound to raise a question of credibility. As Current noted, the story of the carpetbaggers was "told mainly by their enemies." The emotional shock of losing the Civil War had had a great impact on white Southerners, greater even than the physical destruction of the countryside. No conquered people are likely to be cordial toward their conquerors. So embittered were many whites that they absolutely refused to participate in affairs of government even though most of them certainly could have under the reconstruction acts. Though conservatives complained of mass disfranchisements of whites, for example, the evidence indicates that the vast majority could have registered and voted, but did not because they refused to cooperate in any way with the hated Republicans. There were other whites who, after putting their faith in leaders who had led them into a disastrous war, were disillusioned and decided to forsake partisan politics. And there were still others who were too busy cleaning up and rebuilding to care.

The war had brought defeat and humiliation to a proud people. Since defeat and humiliation were not the stuff traditions were made of, the white Southerner found it necessary to reach back and glorify an earlier era in order to find his tradition. Every culture needs a heritage to survive, and the Southerner was no different from anyone else, but since he was the product of a social system that paid special tribute to a romantic past, the defeat in the war was more traumatic to him than it would have been to Northerners whose background was less militaristic and caste-oriented. Americans are told as children that the United States has never lost a war, but the Southerner who looked at his section's history honestly was faced with the fact that *he* had lost a war. To offset this embarrassment, he made the reconstruction a "wailing wall." The more terrible he could make his northern "oppressors" look, the more he could obscure the memory of defeat and justify his violent reaction to radical reconstruction. In addition, not only had he come out of the war a loser, but he had exalted a "cause"—the cause of human bondage—that he now found difficult to defend unless he could make something else appear worse.

Southern whites were also overwhelmed by the prospect of black suffrage, a revolutionary and totally inconceivable idea to most of them. For generations they had been nurtured on the belief that blacks were not good for much else besides picking cotton and chopping cane. "Until the war was over, I think, if there was any one thing I believed stronger and clearer and firmer than another," a fictitious slaveowner lamented in *A Fool's Errand* (1879), a novel by Albion Tourgée, "it was that niggers were made for slaves; and cotton, terbacker, sugar-cane, an' rice, were made for them to raise, and could not be raised in any other way." It was the testimony of such people that historians recorded. But what was really needed was an examination of the carpetbaggers and scalawags themselves to see just who they were and what they did, and with conclusions on black suffrage based on hard facts, not on the reminiscences of racist dreamers like Edward A. Pollard (*The Lost Cause Regained* [1868]) or Henry W. Grady (*The New South* [1890]).

As for the historians themselves, most of the early writers were Southerners who did most of their work in the two decades before World War I. During these years, northern historians, as Larry Kincaid explained in "Victims of Circumstance: An Interpretation of Changing Attitudes Toward Republican Policy Makers and Reconstruction," *Journal of American History* (1970), were relatively indifferent to reconstruction history, considering it something peculiar to the South. The reconstruction, they seemed to say, was the South's private purgatory, best left to southern scholars who were familiar with local mores and institutions. Free to interpret their section's past without contradiction, these historians of redemption portrayed the reconstruction as America's greatest calamity. They were writers with an axe to grind, and when they went looking for evil, they usually found it. They combed the public and private records of the South—memoirs, plantation records, newspapers, state and local archives, and personal interviews with "oldtimers." The state historians of Georgia, Alan Conway told us in *The Reconstruction of Georgia* (1966), "laid bare the bones of Radical reconstruction, analyzing and assessing each minute particle of flesh as it came away for evidence which would damn every aspect of such reconstruction." An intriguing question is why so many people accepted this version for so long.

Perhaps the answer is guilt. Despite all the revisions of reconstruction history, many people still see reconstruction as a "tragic era." Radical reconstruction has always been the great national sin for which Americans have never stopped apologizing. Having defeated the South in battle, Northerners have felt guilty about it ever since and have resigned to the South a victory in fiction that it had lost in fact. The Republicans were evil men, hence Northerners had to purge themselves of the Original Sin of their forebears. To agree with the southern view of reconstruction was an almost masochistic form of penance. Americans, who characteristically refuse to admit to ever having made mistakes, readily confessed to the error of reconstruction because it was entirely a domestic matter. Concomitant to this willingness to confess to the wrongs of reconstruction was an unwillingness to criticize the violent white supremacist reaction to reconstruction. To be sure, the actions of the Ku Klux Klan and other terrorist groups were condemned by the public and the government, but there were many observers who tempered their criticisms by pointing out that the terrorists were only responding to the extremity of Republican evils; thus the Klansmen were not entirely to blame for their conduct. A strong sickness required strong medicine.

THREE

Reconstruction and Race

AFRICANIZATION?

Historians do not much debate the causes of the Civil War any more. When they did, they cited economic differences, constitutional conflict, conspiracy theories, bungling generations, cultural clash, and various other factors. But after the smoke had cleared, the slavery issue still loomed as the greatest single antecedent of the sectional conflict. "All knew that this interest was somehow the cause of the war," Lincoln said in his second inaugural address, almost as if anticipating the historical debate. The same causative relationship existed between the race issue and reconstruction. No matter how the postwar period is dissected and examined, the question of the status of four million former slaves emerges as the most fundamental issue of the conflict. If it is reasonable to say, as Lincoln did, that without slavery there would have been no Civil War, it is also reasonable to say that if there had been no race problem, there would have been no opposition to reconstruction.

It would also probably be more accurate to call it a *racism* problem. In the traditional view of reconstruction, the freedman was portrayed as both a venal politician concerned only with the excitement of the moment and a helpless dupe for the even more venal carpetbaggers and scalawags. But venal politicians are usually too shrewd to be somebody else's dupes, so there is a contradiction in this juxtaposition that the critics have not thought it necessary to reconcile. It really never mattered to the conservatives; the South was being scourged by ne'er-do-wells. In most of the older studies of the reconstruction, such as Claude G. Bowers's *The Tragic Era: The Revolution after Lincoln* (1929), the vast majority of the former slaves were depicted as ignorant pawns molded by unscrupulous Republicans into a powerful voting bloc for the advancement of sinister ends. Where blacks did not actually have a majority, this portrait continued, they supported corrupt Republican machines in each state and, after a significant number of white conservatives had been disfranchised, easily kept the carpetbaggers in power.

Where the freedmen had the numerical majority, the critics went on, they elected administrators and legislators who promptly made a shambles of government. Blacks allegedly seized control of the state governments in South Carolina and Louisiana and brought the legitimate functioning of these states to a complete stop. Their sole aim, whites complained, was to serve their personal desires. "Bowers then proceeded to embroider the theme that Negro rule was widespread, Negro suffrage tragic, and Negro perfidy rampant," one modern historian commented. Many of the older studies include the familiar picture—which is a drawing, not a photograph—of a chamber in the South Carolina legislature where blacks were conducting affairs in what appeared to be chaos, or the equally familiar collection of portraits of the black members of the Louisiana Convention and Assembly of 1868. As scenes of the predominately white legislatures in the other states were rarely shown, it was easy for a reader to conclude that these pictures were typical of the entire South. Such references to black political power also revealed a disturbing assumption on the part of the traditional historians. Though they never came right out and said so (like contemporary whites had), they nonetheless implied that blacks had no right to exercise political power commensurate with their numbers, using as their justification the argument that the former slaves were too ignorant to vote intelligently. The fact that the freedmen constituted almost 40 percent of the South's population seemed not to matter at all.

This portrayal of the freedmen during reconstruction endured as long as the myth of the carpetbaggers—and for the same reasons. Few of the critical scholars bothered to examine the black officeholders themselves to find out just who they were or what they did. Rather, they depended on the observations of whites for their documentation of black reconstruction. Of the efforts to correct this view, historian John Hope Franklin, in three diverse works, took the foremost position: in his brief but illuminating monograph, *Reconstruction: After the Civil War* (1961); in a paper, "Reconstruction and the Negro," in *New Frontiers of the American Reconstruction* (1966); and in a standard text, *From Slavery to Freedom: A History of American Negroes* (revised, 1974). Franklin pointed out that blacks were not as ignorant as they have been traditionally portrayed. There had been many schools throughout the South before the war where, often in violation of the law, slaves had learned to read and write. Numerous slaveowners took the position that laws banning the education of slaves "were for people on other plantations," and "did whatever they pleased regarding their own slaves." Some of the black officeholders were carpetbaggers who had attended northern or European colleges. Of the twenty-two blacks who served in the Congress during the reconstruction, ten had some college and five had degrees, a ratio that was close to that of the white carpetbaggers. One of South Carolina's leading blacks was Robert B. Elliott, who had graduated from Eton in 1859 and could read four languages. Another was Francis L. Cardozo who had studied at the University of Glasgow and in London. The proceedings of the various southern black mutual aid societies also indicated that, although there were few individuals of demonstrated intellect, at least those freedmen who were active in public affairs were "literate people, perfectly capable of thinking through their own problems."

It was not unreasonable to expect black officeholders to have had some formal education, but a more significant event was the extension of basic education to the masses of ex-slaves who were being enfranchised. The most striking effort by the black man to overcome his educational handicap was the system of schools set up by the Freedmen's Bureau. By July 1870, according to Robert Cruden, author of *The Negro in Reconstruction* (1969), the bureau operated 4,239 schools with 9,300 teachers. Though the grades ranged up to college, most of the effort was, understandably, at the elementary level. With free textbooks and no fees, these schools provided some education for over a quarter of a million young and adult former slaves, or about one-sixteenth of the southern black population—an impressive statistic from any standpoint.

In the last analysis, the basis of white opposition to Negro suffrage was not so much a question of black ignorance as of white racism. It was a little curious that so many people should suddenly begin to worry about the educational qualifications of blacks when they had never before complained about enfranchising poorly educated whites. Most of the criticisms of the growing Irish vote in the forties and fifties had been based on religious grounds rather than a genuine concern for an educated electorate. The main theme of the Jacksonian era had been the "rise of the common man," of which the most significant aspect had been the extension of the ballot to all white males, regardless of wealth or education. That this notion had never applied to the commonest man of all was proof of the cultural pervasiveness of white racism in America. It should also be remembered that there had always been a strong resistance to Negro suffrage in the North where blacks had had substantially better educational opportunities. Evidently, the critics of Negro suffrage in the reconstruction objected not to ignorant voters, but to black voters.

A formal education did not, of course, guarantee that there would be no malfeasance among officeholders. But if black politicians in the South were grasping and self-serving—and there is no evidence that they were any more so than anybody else—it might have been because they had had good teachers. For decades southern slaves had been at the bottom of a caste system in which an elitist planter oligarchy manipulated political and economic affairs to suit itself. A small coterie of aristocrats had made most of the important decisions, and the lesser elements, both black and white, had habitually deferred to their "betters." It was intrinsic to the southern "way of life." It was therefore only natural for black politicians in the reconstruction era to use power as they had seen power used. Had not the privileged white man always been the model to which everyone else aspired? Since most of the blacks did not hold their positions of power very long, it appeared that they still had a lot to learn.

One should, furthermore, not make too much of the complaint that blacks outvoted whites throughout the South. Recent scholarship has shown that there was never much real evidence to support the charge that the freedmen were taking over, and, in particular, that southern whites had been disfranchised to guarantee a black majority. Additional research into the election and registration records of individual states and voting districts is needed before a definitive conclusion can be reached. On the basis of the original enrollment of voters, however, the former slaves had registered majorities only in the three states where they constituted over half of the population, plus Florida, where the number of recorded white disfranchisements (less black disfranchisements) was too small to account for the difference, and Alabama, where the number disfranchised was far greater than would have been necessary to assure a simple black majority, suggesting that whites did not register for other reasons. Apparently, most of the eligible southern whites declined to register and vote for various reasons: war-weariness, contempt for Republicans, refusal to appear to approve of black suffrage, disillusionment with politics, and plain indifference. Whatever misery, real or imagined, white Southerners endured, their greatest obstacle was not the black electorate but their own inertia. In fact, once they made up their minds to act, they had little difficulty regaining control of their state governments.

As for black governments, they were entirely a figment of the white man's imagination. For a few years, blacks had a majority in the lower house of the South Carolina legislature; but even here whites usually controlled matters. At no time was there a black majority in any other chamber of any other legislature, and there never was a black governor, despite the fact that three states had black popular majorities. Blacks who held other responsible administrative positions were conspicuous because there were so few of them. Louisiana had three black lieutenant-governors, South Carolina two, and Mississippi one—the three states with black majorities. There were also a few superintendents of education, one state supreme court justice, and one secretary of state. Southern and northern whites cried that the South was being "Africanized," but, if anything, southern blacks were underrepresented. Moreover, it is specious to argue that Americans in the 1860s should not be criticized because the modern "one man, one vote" concept was unfamiliar to them. The House of Representatives had always been organized on that basis; and even the old three-fifths provision of the Constitution, which for almost eighty years had given the South a disproportionate amount of power in the national government, was a recognition of that principle. The simple truth was that most white Americans were racist. They believed blacks were inherently inferior and not entitled to a political voice.

At the local level, blacks did serve in a variety of offices, but, the diversity of city, county, and parish government being what it was, it is impossible to determine the precise significance of blacks as mayors, sheriffs, judges, and so on. Black local government was most extensive and enduring where the black population was most predominant, which was as it should have been. There were many progressive reforms at the local level that long outlasted the black leadership, but some of them were mandated by state authorities, thus there is no way of knowing how much was the result of local efforts. It is instructive that as soon as white conservatives regained control of the state governments, most local black officials found their days numbered. Except in a few instances, black officeholding at the city and county levels was no more secure than it was at the national and state levels. The complaint that the former slaves were seizing control everywhere was groundless, because they seized it nowhere.

In assessing the constructive contributions of black politicians to the general welfare of the South, it can at least be said that they cooperated fully with white Republicans to bring about the reforms already mentioned. Generally, black officeholders were not of high enough rank to be very effective, which was an indictment of their Republican "benefactors" who discouraged them from aspiring to "conspicuous offices." Considering their small numbers, meager resources, and limited experience, it was surprising that black state officials were able to accomplish anything at all. Some historians have noted that blacks elected to Congress contributed little in the way of significant legislation, but these same historians usually ignored the fact that, while black senators and representatives did not introduce any important original legislation, they did support enthusiastically the reform efforts of other Republican members. Through the entire reconstruction era, twenty-two black men served an aggregate of only seven years in the Senate and sixty-four years in the House of Representatives, hardly enough to leave an indelible impression. With so few serving so briefly, it was unrealistic to have expected much in the way of substantial accomplishment. If one went down the congressional role call and picked out the names of any twenty-two men with equivalent training and experience, it is likely that their achievements would be no more impressive.

From this it follows that if the former slaves were not in a position for constructive achievement, they also were not in a position to do all the mischief that whites complained about. Except in a few isolated cases, fears that blacks in power would be vindictive toward their former masters never materialized. Such expectations, of course, were tacit admissions of the iniquity of slavery. Why should whites have feared black vengeance if there was no reason for blacks to be vengeful? Indeed, it is remarkable that there were no major uprisings by the freedmen against the planters. Over the years there had been many examples of slave revolts and interracial genocide in Central and South America and in the Caribbean to inspire black retaliation against whites, and one could argue that the freedmen would have been justified in giving tit for tat. But such was not the case. Throughout the South, blacks made numerous overtures of conciliation, inviting whites to work with them in rebuilding southern society; and in Mississippi, black state legislators petitioned the Congress to remove all the civil disabilities that had been imposed on the former rebel leaders. Needless to say, such efforts were generally spurned by most white Southerners.

LAND AND LABOR

The black incursion into politics was not the only aspect of reconstruction to draw heavy criticism from southern whites. A common complaint was that the freedmen were naturally lazy and that some kind of coercive labor system was imperative. After all, had it not been necessary to drive the slaves continually? Surely, freedom would not change a habit so ingrained and so much a part of the African's nature. In the months following the end of the war many whites, northern as well as southern, commented on the freedmen's apparent lack of initiative. During this period former slaves wandered around the southern countryside, working only when it seemed to suit them. One of the reasons for the black codes, whites contended, was to compel the black man to support himself and his family, otherwise there would be no economic stability and the destitute freedmen would bankrupt the South's meager public resources. Accordingly, vagrancy laws were strictly enforced. Any former slave who could not show some visible means of self-sufficiency was subject to arrest and fine (which he obviously could not pay) or imprisonment. Evidently, no one raised the question of whether the vagrancy laws should apply to indigent whites. As Vernon Lane Wharton wrote in *The Negro in Mississippi, 1865-1890* (1947): "Even if the need of such a strenuous act was accepted, reasons why it should not also apply to unemployed whites could hardly be found."

With respect to the actual extent of black vagrancy, appearances were deceiving. In the first place, the conditions in the immediate postwar South produced a great deal of confusion. Homes had been uprooted, family life had been disrupted, property destruction was widespread, and the roads were clogged with returning Confederate soldiers, many of them crippled or maimed. With such destitution and dislocation, it was only natural that there would be thousands of jobless, homeless refugees, black and white, wandering around looking for some kind of security. It must also be remembered that the freedman was coming out of a lifetime of slavery, hardly the best preparation for independence. Moreover, many blacks were still uncertain of what emancipation meant. Bewildered by the chaos around them and knowing only one kind of existence, they wondered if slavery had indeed been abolished so quickly. The surest way to find out if one could really come and go as he pleased was to "hit the road." Still others went in search of relatives who had been sold before the war. The pathetic sight of a former slave traveling from place to place inquiring about the whereabouts of a wife or son or brother was common. Whatever the reason for the black nomad, the result was a large vagabond population that southern whites blamed on the Negro's "inherent" laziness.

The immediate circumstances of reconstruction aside, there was a more fundamental reason why many freedmen avoided work. For as long as he could remember the slave had worked for nothing. He had grown up believing that work is something one is forced to do. To make the situation bearable, he had developed the art of "getting by," which meant doing as little as possible but enough to keep the master satisfied. Slavery may have been destroyed by the Civil War, but many of its by-products, such as the slave's habit of outwitting his owner by "out-dumbing" him and engaging in a subtle day-to-day rebellion, carried over for many years. "The old masters had vanished quickly and completely," C. Vann Woodward wrote in his introduction to Willie Lee Rose's *Rehearsal for Reconstruction: The Port Royal Experiment* (1964), "but they had left behind them a slave culture and social discipline that was the product of centuries and that would be slow to yield to the newly imported culture of freedom and free enterprise." When one had been forced to labor his entire life for no other reward than being allowed to exist, the temptations of sudden freedom were often impossible to resist.

Furthermore, it was not merely a question of not wanting to work, but of an attitude toward work that had been shaped by 250 years of mental conditioning. In the Old South it had been a widely held notion that gentlemen did not dirty their hands in common labor. The grubby chores of menial occupations fell quite naturally to the ordinary people, especially slaves—the "mudsill" of society, writer George Fitzhugh of Virginia had called them—and poor whites. In reality, many planters, especially those with modest holdings, had worked alongside their slaves. But the *ideal* lifestyle of the gentry had portrayed labor as a demeaning activity, and, as in politics, the great planter had set the style. All of the people who had *worked*, including farmers, tradesmen, professionals, entrepreneurs—and slaves—had endorsed this ideal. When emancipation presented the freedmen with the opportunity to elevate themselves, the most familiar example they had was the great planter. He was the model for perfection, the one whom all others strove to emulate. It was a status symbol not to work.

In view of his experience as a slave, it was also understandable that the freedman would be cynical about being adequately paid for his efforts. Because they expected him to be lazy, it came as a surprise to many whites when they learned that the former slave was industrious if fairly compensated. As early as 1862, freedmen on the Sea Islands along the coast of South Carolina, which had been secured by Union forces in the fall of 1861, had worked without the fear of the lash; and their diligence surprised even their northern white abolitionist supervisors. When freed from the restraints of discrimination, the former slaves could, as Willie Lee Rose pointed out, establish a stable and productive community. "The freedmen had become self-supporting, if not wealthy," she wrote. "They paid their taxes, and they took care of their local troubles with aplomb." Elsewhere, army officers assigned by the War Deaprtment to determine the ex-slaves' readiness to work reported that "the freeman works to accomplish his ends; the slave to end what he is obliged to accomplish." Northern travelers, like John T. Trowbridge, toured the South after the war and agreed that, considering the circumstances, there was very little shirking of responsibility among the former slaves.

The Sea Island experiment had been launched by Northerners sympathetic to the freedmen's plight. When the task of establishing a stable and equitable economy fell to white Southerners, it was an altogether different matter. Some planters did make half-hearted efforts to engage black field workers on a wage-paying basis, but they were largely unsuccessful. When these attempts collapsed, whites were quick to reiterate that the black man was inherently lazy and that some kind of tightly controlled coercive system would have to be established to replace slavery. Such an argument was, of course, self-serving. Despite the complaints of whites, on whom historians depended for assessments of the situation, the evidence indicates that a major cause of the failure of the wage system on the plantations was the universal pessimism of the planters. Most of them had already made up their minds that the former slaves would not be dependable workers under ordinary employment conditions. When one planter's operation broke down, his neighbors became discouraged. Planters who had abandoned the wage system brought pressure on those who were still trying to make it work. Indeed, there was even an abortive attempt in Louisiana to import Chinese field hands so that the growers there would not have to depend on black labor at all!

Admittedly, it would have been difficult, amid the hurly-burly of reconstruction, to start anything new, even with widespread bipartisan support. Thus when the planters jumped at the first chance to give up the wage system and thereby justify their prejudices, the entire effort was doomed to failure. How many of them deliberately undermined it to reinforce their own predispositions cannot be determined. What can be determined is that the tenancy system that eventually took hold in the South, where landowners rented out parcels of their land to individual black farmers in return for a share of the crop, made it possible for white landlords to keep a cheap labor supply on hand indefinitely, which would not have been likely under a wage system. Thus tenancy, defended by whites as only a temporary arrangement until the sharecropper had accumulated enough capital to buy his own farm, became a permanent southern institution. The former slaves were once again tied to the land. Exploited by landlords and merchants, they were in perpetual debt. In some states the descendants of a deceased "cropper" were encumbered by his obligations. Southern states exchanged extradition agreements calling for the return of a tenant who had fled his debts. Slavery returned in all but name.

The problem of acquiring land for the former slaves had been vexing from the start. The freedman did not have the capital to buy any, so he would have to depend on the government. Before the war had ended, rumors circulated widely that the federal authorities were going to break up the large plantations and give each black adult male "forty acres and a mule." But this was the pipe dream of people who had never possessed anything. Proposals to confiscate the estates of former slaveowners and redistribute them to the freedmen never amounted to much, and of those plantations that were seized, most were returned to their owners by decrees of President Johnson. More significantly, many Republicans had mixed feelings about giving the freedman something he ostensibly had not earned. The support for economic aid to blacks came entirely from Republicans, members of a party that held dear the puritan work ethic. People acquired property and personal possessions by working for them, the idea went, not by a handout. Once the slave had been freed, his own enterprise was supposed to be the main factor in his economic progress. It was assumed by whites that all he had to be given was political equality and educational opportunities, historian Robert Cruden explained, and he could then develop the traditional American virtues of "industry, thrift, frugality, sobriety, and self-discipline." But such an expectation "ignored the reality that no matter how good a man's character might be, if he lacked land, capital, and the knowledge of how to use them, he was at the mercy of those who did have them." When the freedmen did not exhibit the desired qualities within the few years since emancipation, many of their so-called benefactors, and most of the general public, fell in with the racist view that their alleged lack of industry was simply part of their African nature.

In addition to the puritan work ethic, the question of land confiscation collided with another cherished American ideal: the sanctity of property rights. It mattered not how a southern planter or his forebears had originally acquired the land—by preferential treatment at government auctions, by outflanking a competitor, by intimidating a poor neighbor, by stealing it from the Indians, or simply by cheating. It mattered even less that they had accumulated most of their great wealth by, in Lincoln's words, "wringing their bread from the sweat of other men's faces." The simple fact was that land titles were defined by state laws. For the national government to interject itself into this matter would open up a whole new can of worms. Nevertheless, the freedman based his claim to the land on the fact that it had been his labor, and the labor of his ancestors, that had made the land valuable. Unlike the European, whose concept of private land ownership dated from the Middle Ages, the African, like the American Indian, had come from a culture where land was in the same category as air and water. God had created it, therefore no individual could claim permanent title to it. One could claim the fruits of his labor—the food he raised on the land—but not the land itself. To those who questioned the freedman's right to the plantation, he simply pointed out that it had been the black slave bent over a hoe or spade who had cleared the trees, dug the wells, picked the cotton, chopped the cane, cultivated the rice, and stacked the tobacco. The slave had *earned* the land.

But this was a rationale that white Americans would not accept. In the first place, the legal principle of usufruct—the right to use and enjoy the benefits of someone else's property without damaging it—was not a part of American common law (although western stockmen grazing cattle on the open range were to make a strong case for it). Secondly, the dogma that property rights were the most hallowed of all human rights was too entrenched, a dogma fortified by the fact that the white man already possessed the land and was unwilling to give it up. The only land the former slaves were able to acquire without great difficulty was public land made available under the Homestead Act of 1862 (much of which had been taken from the Indians), and the shortcomings of that law prevented any large number of blacks (and whites) from successfully and permanently resettling. The Republicans were caught in a paradox. Their party was supposedly committed to the elevation of the black race, to go beyond emancipation; but it was also the political home of the country's strongest supporters of the puritan work ethic and the inviolability of private property. When the dust of reconstruction finally settled, this ambivalence had consigned the black American to a permanent status of economic inequality.

There was also a very pragmatic reason for the Republican resistance to land confiscation. Northern financial interests planning investments in southern industry, agriculture, and railroads opposed proposals to make the freedmen self-sufficient because a guaranteed low-cost labor force was essential to their plans. This put the black man at the center of an economic squeeze. While the entrepreneur wanted a cheap labor supply, the white wage earner objected to black workers for that very reason. For years, one of the most popular northern criticisms of emancipation had been the prediction that thousands of black immigrants would move to nothern cities, glutting the labor market and depressing wages. The only beneficiaries of emancipation, white workers argued, would be the employers. The American trade union movement was still in its infancy in the decade following the Civil War, but it was already beginning to exhibit the white racism that has characterized it ever since. Originally taking a liberal stand on the question of black members (in the view that it needed all the members it could get), the leadership of the National Labor Union, the first national trade union federation in the United States, quickly reversed itself when protests from the white rank and file began pouring in. In effect, the black man was caught between the employers who wanted him denied land so he would remain an exploitable worker, and the white workers who did not want to compete with him. The only circumstance that kept the situation from escalating into a serious labor war was the fact that most of the white wage earners were in the North while most of the potentially menacing black workers remained in the South.

THE MILITANT SOUTH

The successes and failures of Republicans, white and black, were of great significance in determining the course of southern history, and their story is still unfolding. But of more immediate impact was the reaction of white conservatives to congressional reconstruction. Overnight, the war had brought about a revolution in the structure of a society that had steadfastly resisted change. The vast slave population, for so long the "bottom rail" of society, was now demanding an equal share of the rights and privileges claimed by Americans everywhere. At the end of the war southern whites had assumed that the freedmen would become little more than a class of low-paid, unskilled laborers that would remain subservient to whites in all respects. Although emancipation had been a bitter pill, southern whites felt they could live with it. But that was the extent of it. Political and social rights for blacks did not even occur to most southern whites. In other words, Southerners believed that the caste system would continue. Under the Lincoln and Johnson programs, this seemed to be the way things were moving, but when congressional reconstruction descended on the South, the "respectable" conservatives found themselves outvoted. And when southern whites realized they were not going to get their way legally, they resorted to less polite tactics.

It has sometimes been said in defense of the Ku Klux Klan that the men who organized it in late 1865 had no intention of forming a political white terrorist group. Bored by postwar doldrums, they were only looking for a little innocent fun. Yet, as John Hope Franklin pointed out in *Reconstruction: After the Civil War* (1961), it had long been a common practice in Pulaski, Tennessee, for footloose young men with time on their hands to go down to the black settlements and rough up a few "niggers" for the fun of it. The freedmen, of course, were not amused. Still doubtful of their status, they were easily frightened by the night riders. As a slave, the black man had learned that the surest way to survive was to humor the white man, to submit to his abuse, and to be as inconspicuous as possible. Whatever the Klansmen's original motives, it did not take them long to see their opportunity. What began as so-called harmless pranks quickly became organized campaigns of terror and intimidation. Soon related groups began springing up in other parts of the South. Some of them had different names, but they had a common objective and method: the guarantee of white supremacy and the use or threat of violence. Chapters of the Knights of the White Camellia formed in several states; and the White League in Louisiana, the Sons of Washington in Texas, the Society of the White Rose in Mississippi, the Men of Justice in Alabama, the Council of Safety in South Carolina, the Constitutional

Guard and the White Brotherhood in North Carolina, and the Pale Faces in Tennessee, were among the other euphemistically named organizations that complemented, and sometimes overlapped, the Ku Klux Klan.

In January 1869, Grand Wizard Nathan Bedford Forrest, a former Confederate general, disturbed by the rising violence, ordered the Ku Klux Klan disbanded. But it was too late. By this time the Klan's activities had gone beyond its "respectable" national leadership—if it had ever controlled them at all—and the more reckless elements took full charge. Using whatever means necessary, even murder, they broke up Republican meetings, harassed officials of the Freedmen's Bureau, threatened carpetbaggers and others working in the freedmen's behalf, and terrorized blacks until few of them would dare to show their faces on election day. Nor were such tactics confined to night-riding groups. The Klan was supported by whites from virtually every walk of life, Allen W. Trelease pointed out in *White Terror: The Ku Klux Klan Conspiracy and Southern Reconstruction* (1971), and in most states it was practically synonymous with the Democratic party. In the early 1870s, whites in Mississippi implemented what became known throughout the South as the "Mississippi Plan." Eschewing masks and secrecy, local Democrats openly organized themselves into paramilitary forces and marched into black neighborhoods. "They deliberately provoked riots in which hundreds of Negroes were killed," historian Kenneth M. Stampp observed in *The Era of Reconstruction, 1865–1877* (1965), "and they posted armed pickets at registration places to prevent Negroes from registering." Blacks who were bold enough to appear on election day carrying clearly marked Republican ballots "were fired upon or driven away from the polls."

While it is true that only a minority of the southern population engaged in violence, it is nonetheless a commentary on the attitude of a majority of whites that they not only tolerated the terrorists, but, in many instances, welcomed and encouraged them. Amazingly, some whites, though admitting their knowledge of the white supremacist cadres, denied that there had been any violence at all. In later years, southern state governments were to disfranchise the black masses by less violent, though no more subtle, means: white primaries, "grandfather clauses," mass arrests on the day before an election followed by mass releases on the day after, and various social and economic pressures. But in the reconstruction period such sophisticated methods had not yet been devised. Racist fanatics, usually without the machinery of the state government to back them up, relied largely on unrefined force. And to much of the white population, these men were the saviors of the South.

Many Southerners tried to justify the use of terrorism on the grounds that there was no other way of counteracting the hated black militia units that had been raised by Republican politicians in some southern states. White conservatives claimed that black militiamen were nothing more than mercenaries for corrupt Republican state regimes and personal bodyguards for carpetbaggers. Whatever truth there was to their complaint, their hatred of the black militia went much deeper than that. In the first place, whites were piqued by the sight of a black man in uniform, occupying a position of rank and authority. In the southern tradition, this was a privilege reserved for the "well-born." More significantly, many whites, clinging to the stereotype of the "savage African," were terrified by the sight of an armed Negro. If the black man suddenly acquired power, his primitive, barbaric instincts would surface, they cried. The result would be a rampage of rape, murder, arson, pillage, and all sorts of unspeakable offenses. In the absence of a "responsible" (meaning white conservative) state government, whites claimed that they had no choice but to resort to vigilantism—a traditional American way of enforcing law and order.

But such a reaction was just another example of racist hysteria. Of the eleven former Confederate states, only seven raised militia units, and only four of these enrolled substantial numbers of blacks. Open to men from 18 to 40 years of age, the militia units appealed to many young black men, attracted by the uniform, the guaranteed wage, and the idea that they would be doing something to ensure their freedom. Had the white critics taken a closer look at the so-called black militias, they would have seen that many of them were predominately white, none of them was all black, and that all of the commanders, who had been appointed by the governors, were white. But, as southern historian Otis A. Singletary put it in *Negro Militia and Reconstruction* (1957), "the longstanding Southern indifference to logic" meant that, just as a discernible drop of black blood made an otherwise white person all black, all a militia unit needed to be branded a Negro unit was one Negro.

Despite efforts to explain it as a phenomenon of the moment, violence against blacks was much more deeply rooted. The South had had a long history of violence and resort to arms. As Franklin explained in *The Militant South, 1800–1861* (1956), "In the ante-bellum period, large numbers of observers, including Southerners, made more than passing reference to those phases of Southern life and culture that suggested a penchant for militancy which at times assumed excessive proportions." There were numerous reasons for this, most of them obvious: the South had gone through a longer frontier period with the threat of Indian warfare; plantation society lived by the martial code of the cavalier under which great planters saw themselves as members of a privileged gentry; the South was a closed society and with the ruling class complacent, its members were belligerent toward change. Certainly most important of all was the existence of chattel slavery. By its very nature, slavery required a stern hand for its continued existence. Caste societies are compelled to rely on force and the threat of physical punishment to thwart encroachments from below; they cannot survive otherwise and remain caste societies.

Many of these factors manifested themselves in the Civil War. It was no accident that the southern states had always sent a disproportionately large number of their young men to the United States Military Academy at West Point. Before (and since) the war, military academies ranging from elementary grades through the collegiate level—"West Points of the South," Franklin called them—were more numerous and played a larger role in southern life than similar schools elsewhere. They were a conspicuous indication of the mystique of the uniform that fascinated southern whites from all walks of life. While northern young men were venturing into farming, manufacturing, commerce, banking, land speculation, and internal improvements, their southern counterparts, without the same access to land and capital and discouraged from enterprises alien to the southern monoculture, pursued the few courses open to them—the law and the military—which launched many of them into political careers. The upshot of this was that when the war began, most of the best U.S. Army officers were Southerners who returned to their home states and became the nucleus of the Confederate officer corps. They could have remained in the United States Army without compromising their commitment to a military way of life, so their defection suggests that they were really more dedicated to the *southern* way of life. Additionally, southern enlisted men were, on the whole, more familiar with guns and horses and more accustomed to life in the field than northern soldiers. After generations during which the middling folk habitually deferred to their "betters," southern soldiers were also more conditioned to following orders without questioning the reasons for them. Taken together, these factors were significant in the early Confederate victories.

A less conspicuous but equally significant source of the southern impulse for violence was the persistence of the *code duello*. Although dueling had been outlawed throughout the country long before the Civil War, it had always had a special allure in the South and was illegally practiced there for many years, often with the authorities looking the other way. As Franklin noted, "In a section where laws were casually regarded and indifferently enforced, it was too much to expect that legislatures could merely write off dueling." Nor was it confined to short-tempered young men, but, as an honored tradition among "gentlemen," found favor among some of the South's leading citizens. Dueling had virtually disappeared by the Civil War, but the attitude that had nurtured the earlier proclivity for it remained. Accordingly, the ease with which respectable members of southern society disregarded antidueling laws carried over into the reconstruction period in the actions of those defenders of white supremacy who defied laws they did not like.

In view of all this, it should come as no surprise that the use of physical force to resolve a problem would be a common practice in the South during the reconstruction era. The Civil War had forced white Southerners to make revolutionary changes in their way of doing things, but it could not force revolutionary changes in their way of thinking.

THE BETRAYAL
OF THE FREEDMEN

The year 1870 was a significant one for the black American because it marked the peak of the public concern over his welfare. It was fortuitous that the Republicans went for the Fifteenth Amendment when they did because a new movement was emerging within the party that did not augur well for the freedmen. Dishonesty in public office was reaching epidemic proportions, with more still to come; thus it was only a matter of time until concerned party members began calling for reform, if for no other reason than to keep the Democrats from capitalizing on the issue. The corruption in the administration, which President Grant seemed to have no inclination to stop, the questionable activities of some congressmen who were receiving favors for supporting proposals beneficial to special interests, and the graft and widespread abuse of office at the state and local levels in both North and South, began to attract public attention away from the race issue and other matters related to the war. In 1870, Republicans in Missouri, led by Carl Schurz, launched a reform program that was to become the Liberal Republican movement. Spreading to other states and finally into national politics, the movement reached its climax in 1872 when former radicals like Schurz, Sumner, and Theodore Tilton repudiated the regular Republican organization and nominated their own presidential candidate, editor Horace Greeley of the

New York *Tribune*, on a platform of honesty in government and civil service reform. Greeley's campaign slogan was, appropriately, "Turn the Rascals Out!"

In the last analysis, the Liberals did serious damage to the cause of the freedmen, a consequence which belied their pronounced commitment to liberalism—even in nineteenth-century terms. They supported the Fourteenth and Fifteenth Amendments, but they also called for an end to congressional reconstruction and the federal military presence in the South—without which the remaining Republican state governments would quickly fall. "To these disenchanted men the radical governments had failed," Stampp explained, "the Negro as a freedman had been a disappointment, and home rule under the old white leadership was the only way to restore honest government." That these former supporters of emancipation and impartial suffrage could change so quickly underscored the insidiousness of white racism in America. Four million former slaves had known freedom for barely seven years, during which every conceivable obstacle was thrown in their way, but some of their white "friends" were already giving up because the freedmen were taking so long to become part of the American mainstream. The Liberal betrayal was also a strong reminder that many, perhaps most, Republicans had not supported black suffrage for moral reasons, but for selfish ones, and their plea for the reestablishment of white home rule in the South in order to eliminate corruption was in total disregard of the fact that dishonest politicians had flourished in the Old South and were certain to flourish in the New South as well.

The Democratic party, devoid of effective leadership, also supported Greeley, but he lost anyway. The Liberal Republican movement faded faster than it had emerged, but the damage it had done to the cause of racial equality endured.

To most white Americans the ratification of the Fifteenth Amendment in March 1870, meant that the antislavery movement had finally come to an end. The three great amendments had reconstituted the fabric of American society. They had freed the slave, granted him equal protection of the laws, and guaranteed him the right to vote. The freedman now had the necessary tools to establish himself as an equal member of society, whites argued, and therefore what happened from now on was up to him. If he failed to prosper he would have no one to blame but himself; the white man had done all he could. At the same time, the notion that the race problem was peculiar to the South and should thus be handled by Southerners was gaining widespread favor in the North. The fact that Northerners considered the former slaves as the problem was one more example of their racism. Questions of morality, of right and wrong, of civil rights, or of human dignity and worth, seemed not to matter in the racist line of reasoning. The "Negro problem" was seen as one for southern *whites* to solve, a complete denial of the fact that the southern white *was* the problem. It was the white man who disdained interracial cooperation, scorned outside influence, defied federal law, and approved the use of violence against the blacks. The source of the conflict in the South was not the presence of blacks, as everyone universally assumed, but the white Southerner's racism; and it was to *him* that Northerners now consigned the resolution of the "race problem." What many northern whites later convinced themselves was the return of racial harmony in the South was in reality the return of racial subjugation.

The growing public apathy in the North over reconstruction and the waning interest of the freedmen's friends in the national government were easily exploited by the southern old guard. As early as October 1869, the Republican government in Tennessee, in power since 1865, was deposed by conservatives, and in the same month similar forces won control of the Virginia state government and took office the following January. On November 30, 1870, conservatives won control of North Carolina, an action repeated in Georgia almost exactly one year later. Republicans lost control of Texas in 1873, and conservatives in Arkansas and Alabama returned to power in 1874. Following the elections in Mississippi in the fall of 1875, only three former Confederate states—Florida, South Carolina, and Louisiana— still had Republican governments, holdovers made possible by the presence of federal bayonets that would shortly be bartered away. 93

The end of reconstruction was a classic study in political and economic expediency. In the presidential election of 1876, the Democratic candidate, Samuel J. Tilden of New York, had a clear popular majority and appeared to have an electoral majority as well over his Republican opponent, Rutherford B. Hayes of Ohio. But the returns in three southern states, which, interestingly, were the states where Republicans were still in control, were challenged by supporters of Hayes. The result was a dispute over nineteen electors, all of which Hayes would have to have in order to win the presidency. The situation could not have been more dramatic had it been contrived by an overimaginative playwright. As it stood, Tilden had 184 electors and Hayes had 166, with 185 needed to win. "The three disputed Southern states now became the object of a tug of war," as James G. Randall and David Donald put it in *The Civil War and Reconstruction* (revised, 1961), "in which both contestants resorted to the most unscrupulous methods." When both slates of electors in each state voted on December 6, supporters of each candidate claimed victory. To complicate matters, both the Democratic-controlled House of Representatives and the Republican-controlled Senate had appointed investigating committees, which submitted predictable reports. So urgent was the situation that the Congress finally created a special electoral commission made up of five representatives, five senators, and five justices of the Supreme Court to decide who had won. The commission had a majority of Republicans and it proceeded to assign all of the disputed electors, and the presidency, to Hayes.

The traditional version of the election of 1876 has it that Tilden was cheated out of the presidency, but an analysis of the returns raises a strong doubt. While it appears that Republican election officials in the three disputed states were indeed guilty of tampering with returns, it is equally evident that thousands of blacks in all of the former Confederate states, most of whom would have voted for Hayes, had been frightened away from the polls or otherwise prevented from voting. Democrats were quick to complain of the former, but unwilling to acknowledge the latter; and, until recently, historians generally went along because the misbehavior of the Republicans was part of the traditional story of reconstruction, while the intimidation of black voters was not. In short, had the election been conducted fairly on all fronts, Hayes probably would have been the winner anyway.

Moreover, the explanation of why the Democrats eventually agreed to accept the special commission's decision was similarly misjudged by historians. In February 1877, less than a month before the constitutionally mandated date on which a new president is sworn into office, several southern Democrats and influential northern Republicans met at the Wormley Hotel in Washington, D.C. (owned, ironically, by a black businessman), and struck a compromise in which the South would not challenge Hayes's election in return for an assurance from Hayes that the federal troops would be removed from the three southern states still under Republican control. The Wormley bargain has received a great deal of attention by historians because it was well-publicized and well-timed, and subsequent events gave it credence. It was all so logical. It also might have been a smokescreen. Whatever the motivation behind it, it diverted attention away from what was a far more important development. Hayes was already committed to withdrawing the remaining troops from the South; and even if he had not been, with white conservatives chipping away at what was left of southern Republican leadership, it would only have been a question of time before he did so. Besides, Tilden certainly would have done the same thing. There was really no reason why the South should compromise on this point because the Hayes supporters had no bargaining strength.

What was far more important than a presidential assurance of white home rule in three states was, as C. Vann Woodward explained in his illuminating *Reunion and Reaction: The Compromise of 1877 and the End of Reconstruction* (1956), a sympathetic ear when it came to government assistance for southern economic development. Still recovering from the devastation of the war and reeling under the depression that followed the panic of 1873, the southern economy remained backward and vulnerable to sudden changes. Many southern whites were convinced that the North's industrial power had been the key to its victory in the Civil War, and that the South would continue to lag behind the North in economic progress as long as it clung to a monoculture. Thus what really emerged out of the Compromise of 1877 was the launching of the New South—a commitment to industrialization, railroads, mineral exploration, technology, and urbanization. The North had already begun to unleash a tremendous burst of industrial energy and would continue to make enormous gains in economic growth in the decades following the reconstruction. The best way to assure the same success in the South was to secure the kind of financial backing that only federal assistance could generate. With the attraction of government subsidies, private investment would not be far behind—which was one reason why so many northern businessmen were anxious for a sectional reconciliation. It should be remembered that the move to elect Hayes with the promise of financial aid was not a last-minute desperation effort, but was the culmination of an elaborate plan that had been set in motion the instant it appeared Hayes had lost the election. The Republicans looked for the southern Achilles' heel and found it. When northern Democrats moved to block the special commission's decision, they suddenly found themselves deserted by their southern brethren. And the reconstruction was over.

THE LEGACY
OF RECONSTRUCTION

Wars are events of extreme opposites, with heroes and villains, allies and enemies, winners and losers. In a foreign war the enemy is easy to isolate and identify because he is usually different in so many ways: language, customs, traditions, economic and political systems, etc. Often he is geographically remote. Neutrality is difficult but possible. It is the singular characteristic of a civil war that the citizens of a country are fighting among themselves, and that therefore few of these factors are present. And neutrality is impossible. After an international war the victors may find it easy, and even desirable, to be magnanimous toward the vanquished; and even if they are oppressive, there is always the hope that they can be driven out. But in the American Civil War the two sides were supposed to resume living together harmoniously, with the losers expected to be contrite and do most of the adjusting. The conflict had the characteristics of a family feud in which hatreds were passed from one generation to the next with the principals unable to remember why everyone was still fighting.

Nor were the victors free from highly charged emotions. Since a civil war is a rebellion against established authority, the onus of treason is always present. One can respect the integrity of a foreign enemy because he at least appears to be fighting for a patriotic ideal that he presumably believes in. While this may also be true in a civil war, it is hard for the side that is rebelled against to see it. In the American Civil War the presence of men from the same state in opposing armies underlined this situation. After the war, more than a few angry Northerners expressed the opinion that the secessionist leaders should be summarily executed as traitors. It was of the greatest significance that in the United States the worst elements of both a civil war and a foreign war were present. The war had the bitterness of an internal rebellion, but it was fought between two societies that were in many respects as different as two independent nations. Under these circumstances, any postwar adjustment was bound to be painful.

Moreover, since the reconstruction was so inextricably bound up with moral issues, it was difficult to be thoroughly objective about it—assuming that objectivity was desirable. The fact that one was born or educated in one region of the nation did much to influence his bias. The problem was dramatized by foreign observers who, it would seem, had no axe to grind, but who nonetheless usually favored one view. In reporting on his postwar travels in the United States in *American Reconstruction,*

1865–1870: And the Impeachment of President Johnson (1928 [1865–1870]), the young French medical student, Georges Clemenceau, was openly sympathetic to the radical Republicans. Nor did the historical detachment that can be expected to come with the perspective of time assure neutrality. In 1963, British historian W. R. Brock admitted to looking at the problems of reconstruction "through northern eyes," and made a good part of his preface to *An American Crisis: Congress and Reconstruction, 1865–1867* a rejoinder to expected criticism.

When it came to polarizing sectional attitudes, the reconstruction was thus the most influential single episode in American history, especially for southern whites. Memorials to boys in gray were as much a wish for what might have been as a tribute to their courage. Paeans of battlefield heroics and laments to Confederate dead were, in fact, songs of mourning and could have been sung by Northerners as well. Even romantic allusions to the so-called glories of the Old South were usually little more than nostalgic glances backward to the pleasures of plantation life, pleasures that only a small fraction of the population enjoyed. But when the subject of reconstruction was broached to members of the postwar generation and most of its descendants, the first reaction was one of anger and resentment. It was a paradox. Unlike the war, the reconstruction caused no major loss of life, no widespread property destruction, and no permanent dislocation of political leadership. Indeed, as we have seen, there were numerous benefits. Yet it was the reconstruction, and not the war, that became the great catalyst of southern sectional allegiance.

The end result was a conservative, one-party South committed to the perpetuation of white supremacy. Thus, although the black man did not dominate the South, as so many whites had fearfully predicted, he did dominate the South's thinking. Politicians quickly learned that the surest way to get elected was to "out-nig" the opposition. The reconstruction also left the South with a casual attitude toward law and order, especially when the race issue was involved. Whites traditionally resented "outside agitators," and the cry of "states' rights" is still heard occasionally from segregationists and others trying to obstruct the enforcement of federal laws and court decisions. At the same time, the black man learned from the reconstruction experience that he would have to look to the national government for the protection of his rights, because he was not going to find it at the state level. To him, local self-government was a euphemism for black disfranchisement. The knowledge that southern law was the white man's law—and would be enforced to suit the white man—understandably produced among blacks a strong disrespect for it. The modern black's contempt for law enforcement agencies, in the South and elsewhere, goes back at least to the reconstruction period and is the chief product of a century of legal double standards.

Finally, the reconstruction was also the end of what was nothing less than a classic revolution. To be sure, the use of the name "Jacobin" to identify radical Republicans was common in the Democratic press. An aggressive minority faction had demanded fundamental changes that conservatives resisted. When moderates grew disenchanted over the president's unwillingness to consider even the most reasonable reconstruction proposals, they joined the radicals in overruling him and attempting to overthrow him. The element of force was present in the creation of the military districts, and to a lesser degree in the Republican southern state militias. The culmination of the revolutionary crusade was the impeachment trial. Though the attempt to convict failed, it did succeed in removing the president as a factor in the reconstruction process. But it also, in Brock's words, belonged "to that class of gambles in which revolutionary movements characteristically overplay their hands." The revolutionaries triumphed, but they also went too far, as revolutionaries are wont to do, and a conservative reaction set in.

But it can be argued with equal force that the revolutionaries failed, that the reconstruction was indeed a "tragic era" because the radicals did not go far enough. As Grady McWhiney put it in "Reconstruction: Index of Americanism," in *The*

Southerner as American (1960), "The tragedy of Reconstruction was that it did not really reconstruct." Most of the reformers had seen emancipation and reconstruction as the *end* of a reform era. Blacks and the few people who still argued their cause, on the other hand, saw reconstruction as the *beginning* of a new era of social and political equality—but they were in no position to put their desires into action. Landless, powerless, politically impotent, disorganized, and economically dependent on white employers and landlords, blacks could only sit and watch the promises of reconstruction disintegrate. The radical Republicans had been brutalized by their own rise to power and, increasingly, reformers grew disillusioned with politics as an instrument of humanitarianism.

Even without the failure of impeachment, radicalism would have declined rapidly. The emergence of men like Stevens, Sumner, and Wade was not an *ad hoc* phenomenon, but was the last phase of abolition, a far-reaching reform movement that had begun four decades earlier. The Civil War was the movement's most violent expression, and the reconstruction was its aftermath. As in most revolutionary aftermaths, an emotional letdown occurred; people simply grew tired of slogans and moral entreaties. Many of the original revolutionary leaders died or grew old and weary, and the younger men who came up had different ideas. Stevens, Sumner, and Wade were succeeded by men like Roscoe Conkling, James G. Blaine, and James A. Garfield, whose vision for America was anything but revolutionary. Moreover, many reformers had been idealists, committed to principles that were supposed to produce a perfect world. When things did not work out as they had hoped, they became disenchanted, indifferent, and even bitter.

If radical reconstruction is viewed as the last gasp of a sweeping revolutionary movement, the desperation that distinguished its final hours can be understood. There was still a large enough reform element in the Congress to pass the Civil Rights Act of 1875, a measure prohibiting racial discrimination in places of public accommodation and in jury selection, but this eleventh-hour action was taken under a cloud of finality. It would be three-fourths of a century before Congress would again enact significant civil rights legislation.

Bibliographical Essay

The need for a reassessment of the reconstruction was pointed out sooner than many historians have been willing to admit. Black scholars like W. E. B. DuBois in his "Reconstruction and Its Benefits," *American Historical Review* (1910), and Alrutheus A. Taylor, with *The Negro in South Carolina during Reconstruction* (1924), *The Negro in the Reconstruction of Virginia* (1926), and *The Negro in Tennessee, 1865–1880* (1938), had made it clear that the standard view was incomplete and in many respects incorrect. In 1938 the *Journal of Negro History* published two articles—Taylor's "Historians of the Reconstruction" and Horace Mann Bond's "Social and Economic Forces in Alabama Reconstruction"—which again called attention to the deficiencies of the traditional interpretation. But it was not until 1939, when *white* historians began reexamining reconstruction, that the matter began to become the subject of extensive revisionist attention. Francis B. Simkin's "New

Viewpoints of Southern Reconstruction," *Journal of Southern History* (1939), and Howard K. Beale's "On Rewriting Reconstruction History," *American Historical Review* (1940), paved the way for later essays like T. Harry Williams's "An Analysis of Some Reconstruction Attitudes," *Journal of Southern History* (1946), John Hope Franklin's "Whither Reconstruction Historiography," *Journal of Negro Education (1948)*, and Bernard Weisberger's "The Dark and Bloody Ground of Reconstruction Historiography," *Journal of Southern History* (1959). Reconstruction historiography has come 180 degrees from its original position, but Thomas J. Pressly, in "Racial Attitudes, Scholarship, and Reconstruction: A Review Essay," *Journal of Southern History* (1966), has, in an obvious allusion to the zeal of modern liberal reform, judiciously cautioned against "potential distortions . . . arising from . . . ideological convictions."

One barometer of the intensity of a historical debate is the increase in the number of anthologies featuring essays by proponents of opposing sides. One of the first works of this kind is *Reconstruction in the South* (1952) edited by Edwin C. Rozwenc for the *Problems in American Civilization* (Amherst) series. Then, after a long interlude, the pace quickened with Harold M. Hyman's *New Frontiers of the American Reconstruction* (1966), a series of provocative papers read at a conference in 1965 at the University of Illinois. Charles Crowe's *The Age of Civil War and Reconstruction, 1830–1900: A Book of Interpretative Essays* was also published in 1966, but only the final thirteen of its forty-two selections pertain to the reconstruction. In 1967 Staughton Lynd's small volume, *Reconstruction*, was published; followed by a similar work edited by Seth M. Scheiner, *Reconstruction: A Tragic Era?* (1968), a volume in Holt, Rinehart, and Winston's *American Problem Studies* that focuses on the debate over the errors of reconstruction. Richard O. Curry's *Radicalism, Racism, and Party Realignment: The Border States during Reconstruction* (1969) is a collection of nine original essays dealing primarily with internal politics in six border states. The most ambitious work is *Reconstruction: An Anthology of Revisionist Writings* (1969), edited by Kenneth M. Stampp and Leon F. Litwack. This volume is made up of twenty-two essays from revisionist articles and books, some of which are cited elsewhere in this critique.

Of the recent general histories, David Donald's 1961 revision of James G. Randall's *The Civil War and Reconstruction* (1937), is still one of the best accounts—although many of its original biases remain. One can only wish that the authors had divided their attention more equally between the 4-year war (534 pages) and the 12-year reconstruction (167 pages). A more recent general history is Avery Craven's *Reconstruction: The Ending of the Civil War* (1969), which, though revisionist, is a restrained work that suffers from the author's determination merely to "see men and situations in their own time and place" and to withhold judgments on right and wrong. Rembert W. Patrick, in *The Reconstruction of the Nation* (1967), places southern reconstruction in the larger context of the national scene. A leading general text of southern history since the Civil War is John Samuel Ezell's *The South since 1865* (1963), the first 114 pages of which present a balanced summary of the reconstruction. Despite these recent efforts, the revisionist viewpoint is most compellingly presented in concise interpretative monographs, two of which are John Hope Franklin's *Reconstruction: After the Civil War* (1961), which emphasizes the accomplishments of the freedmen; and Kenneth M. Stampp's *The Era of Reconstruction, 1865–1877* (1965), which focuses on the political aspects of the period.

Although the revisionists have clearly won the day, students of reconstruction would do well to consult the older works for at least two reasons: first, familiarity with the changes in historical interpretation that occur over a period of time enables the reader to appreciate the problems of critical analysis and the axiom that history is not what has happened but what historians have said has happened. Second, a comparison of works from different periods illustrates the influence of the political climate and social mood of the historian's own time. William A. Dunning's two best-known works, *Essays on the Civil War and Reconstruction* (1897, revised, 1904) and *Reconstruction: Political and Economic, 1865–1877* (1907)—both available in modern paperback editions—appeared at a point in American history when the status of blacks was at its lowest and racialism was a dominant theme in the nation's foreign policy. A few years later, with black and white civil libertarians beginning to organize, *The Facts of Reconstruction* (1914) was published, a reply to the racist Dunning historians written by John R. Lynch, a former southern black legislator. After World War I, as the pendulum swung back to the right, the reactionary era of the twenties was the setting for the writing of Claude G. Bowers's bitterly antiradical *The Tragic Era: The Revolution after Lincoln* (1929). But on the eve of the New Deal era, Francis B. Simkins and Robert H. Woody published *South Carolina during Reconstruction* (1932), a significant break away from the Dunning thesis. Two Marxist—and, therefore, doctrinaire— interpretations, W. E. B. DuBois's *Black Reconstruction: An Essay toward a History of the Part Which Black Folk Played in the Attempt to Reconstruct Democracy in America, 1860–1880* (1935) and James Allen's *Reconstruction: The Battle for Democracy, 1865–1877* (1937), were published during the Great Depression when radical economic themes were popular. Also stressing economic and social matters is Paul H. Buck's *The Road to Reunion, 1865–1900* (1937), which portrays the postwar era as one of the reestablishment of sectional harmony; but it is a book in which the author exhibited the typical white racist posture by ignoring the fact that such harmony was achieved at the expense of the southern black population for whom life was anything but harmonious. More in accord with the traditional view is Ralph Selph Henry's *The Story of Reconstruction* (1938). The work of E. Merton Coulter, *The South during Reconstruction, 1865–1877* (1947), in the multivolume *The History of the South*, is best described as the last of the old interpretations; while Hodding Carter's *The Angry Scar: The Story of Reconstruction* (1959) is not a scholarly analysis but a superficial description by a southern journalist.

Since most of the older state studies inspired by Dunning have long been out of print and can only be found in university and large public libraries, it would be somewhat pointless to list them here. A few, however, can be reviewed for purposes of comparison with more recent works. James W. Garner's *Reconstruction in Mississippi* (1901), which has been reprinted in paperback (1968) and therefore is widely available, should be read along with Vernon Lane Wharton's *The Negro in Mississippi, 1865–1890* (1947) and William C. Harris's *Presidential Reconstruction in Mississippi* (1967). Similarly, Edwin C. Wooley's *The Reconstruction of Georgia* (1901) and C. Mildred Thompson's *Reconstruction in Georgia, Economic, Social, Political, 1865–1872* (1915) can be compared with profit to Allan Conway's *The Reconstruction of Georgia* (1966) and Elizabeth Studley Nathan's *Losing the Peace: Georgia Republicans and Reconstruction, 1865–1871* (1968)—though the latter volume is restricted in scope. Thomas B. Alexander's *Political Reconstruction in Tennessee* (1950) is the only book dealing with the whole range of issues in one state that was published before the Supreme Court's desegregation decision of 1954—the starting point of what some have called the "Second Reconstruction." The more recent works have, like Wharton's, focused on the freedmen, as exemplified by two books published in 1965: Joe M. Richardson's *The Negro in the Reconstruction of Florida, 1865–1877* and Joel Williamson's *After Slavery: The Negro in South Carolina during Reconstruction, 1861–1877*.

None of these works, however, blazes any new trails in their attention to the former slaves. Black historian Alrutheus A. Taylor, between 1924 and 1938, published the three works cited above. But, as with the works of DuBois, Carter Woodson, and Horace Mann Bond, Taylor's findings were largely ignored by white historians who did not think that black scholars could possibly have anything important to say.

Many of the most perceptive revisionist studies of the reconstruction era deal with the period preceding the triumph of the radicals and the advent of congressional reconstruction in 1867. Some of these works focus on the exigencies of wartime reconstruction and the conflict between the president, as commander-in-chief of the Union armies, and the Congress, as the arbiter of relations between the states and the national government. William B. Hesseltine's *Lincoln's Plan of Reconstruction* (1960, reprinted in 1967 with an introduction by Richard N. Current) is the standard work on that subject; but the definitive study of the debate during the war years is Herman Belz's *Reconstructing the Union: Theory and Policy during the Civil War* (1969), which recreates in minute detail the intense—almost vicious—infighting between representatives of opposing viewpoints. David Donald's *The Politics of Reconstruction, 1863–1867* (1965), a brief but fascinating account of congressional voting patterns, is, with its numerous statistical tables, one of the first significant applications of quantitative historical methodology to a noneconomic Civil War subject. On the marshaling of forces and the inevitable collision between Andrew Johnson and the radicals, LaWanda and John H. Cox's *Politics, Principle, and Prejudice, 1865–1866: Dilemma of Reconstruction America* (1963) is a major study; while W. R. Brock, in his *An American Crisis: Congress and Reconstruction, 1865–1867* (1963) has provided the perspective of a foreign observer. Both of these works cast new light on the internal struggle for leadership among conservatives, moderates, and radicals within the Republican party. With Johnson himself as the central figure, Eric McKitrick's *Andrew Johnson and Reconstruction* (1960) is the major revisionist study of the embattled seventeenth president. Seeing Johnson as primarily a victim of his own weaknesses, McKitrick has controverted the basic assumptions of earlier works by Howard K. Beale, *The Critical Year: A Study of Andrew Johnson and Reconstruction* (1930), and George Fort Milton, *The Age of Hate: Andrew Johnson and the Radicals* (1930), both of which viewed the president as the unfortunate victim of an insidious radical conspiracy. Milton Lomask's *Andrew Johnson: President on Trial* (1960) is, though marred by journalistic flippancy and an avuncular affection for his subject, the most detailed study of the impeachment proceedings. Since he chose to quote so heavily, one can only wish that he had chosen to cite his sources.

A great deal has been written about the radical Republicans, most of it unfavorable. It has only been in recent years that the members of this zealous faction have been viewed as something less than villains— as idealistic but fallible, realistic but passionate, altruistic but corruptible, virtuous but capable of mendacity—a view which owes a great deal to the currency of the racial issue in American life today. This emerging portrait of the radicals is carefully analyzed by Larry Kincaid in "Victims of Circumstance: An Interpretation of Changing Attitudes toward Republican Policy Makers and Reconstruction," *Journal of American History* (1970). More has probably been written about the radicals in books and articles than in biographies, but a few of the latter stand out. Fawn Brodie's *Thaddeus Stevens: Scourge of the South* (1959) and Milton Meltzer's *Thaddeus Stevens and the Fight for Negro Rights* (1967) are two sympathetic, but not effusive, treatments of the Pennsylvania congressman whose scowling portrait was so long the symbol of all radicalism. Charles Sumner's postwar career is admirably revealed in David Donald's not uncritical *Charles Sumner and the Rights of Man* (1970), the sequel to his Pulitzer Prize–winning study of Sumner and the coming of the Civil War. In a work begun by Benjamin P. Thomas and completed by Harold M. Hyman, Edwin M. Stanton's role has been meticulously reviewed in *Stanton: The Life and Times of Lincoln's Secretary of War* (1962). Since Stanton started out as a Jacksonian Democrat and had been Buchanan's attorney-general during the secession crisis, a study of his conversion to radicalism is especially illuminating in understanding the decade after the war. An excellent work is Hans L. Trefousse's *Benjamin F. Wade: Radical Republican from Ohio* (1963), a sound, scholarly study that did much to enhance the image of the radicals generally. A more comprehensive work on this theme and one which should stand as the definitive study on the radicals for some time is Trefousse's *The Radical Republicans: Lincoln's Vanguard for Racial Justice* (1969); and the radicals are also viewed favorably in Martin E. Mantell's *Johnson, Grant, and the Politics of Reconstruction* (1973).

The economic view of Republican motivation, pioneered by Charles A. and Mary Beard in *The Rise of American Civilization* (2 vols., 1927), has come in for sharp criticism by modern scholars. The most recent standard work supporting the Beardian interpretation is George R. Woolfolk's *The Cotton Regency: The Northern Merchants and Reconstruction, 1865–1880* (1958). Opposing this view and taking the position that the Republicans were less motivated by economic interests than humanitarian ones, are Robert P. Sharkey, *Money, Class, and Party: An Economic Study of the Civil War and Reconstruction* (1950); Stanley Coben, "Northeastern Business and Radical Reconstruction: A Re-Examination," *Mississippi Valley Historical Review* (1959); and Irwin Unger, "Business Men and Specie Resumption," *Political Science Quarterly* (1959). An intriguing work which also disputes the Beardian view and sees class conflict as the "submerged shoal on which Radical dreams [of equality before the law] foundered," is David Montgomery's *Beyond Equality: Labor and the Radical Republicans, 1862–1872* (1967).

With reconstruction revisionism shifting from the general to the specific, the carpetbaggers and scalawags are sure to be the subjects of research in the coming years. Jack B. Scroggs, in "Carpetbagger Constitutional Reform in the South Atlantic States, 1867–1868," *Journal of Southern History* (1961), was one of the first scholars to suggest that perhaps the carpetbaggers, like the radicals, were not all that bad. A sympathetic look at a major carpetbagger is Otto H. Olsen's biography, *Carpetbagger's Crusade: The Life of Albion Winegar Tourgée* (1965). Richard N. Current has done as much as anyone to construct a balanced view in "Carpetbaggers Reconsidered," *A Festschrift for Frederick B. Artz* (1964); and *Three Carpetbag Governors* (1967), a candid review of the careers of Harrison Reed, Henry Clay Warmoth, and Adelbert Ames. What is really needed are a lot more studies like William C. Harris's "The Creed of the Carpetbaggers: The Case of Mississippi," *Journal of Southern History* (1974), which goes a long way toward destroying the myth of the carpetbaggers. And yet, despite this need, W. C. Nunn's *Texas under the Carpetbaggers* (1962), with its almost exclusive reliance on southern white sources and older secondary works, can only be described as a throwback to the Dunning era. David Donald first called attention to the need for a fresh look at the scalawags in "The Scalawag in Mississippi Reconstruction," *Journal of Southern History* (1944). The thesis that the scalawags drew much of their strength from the old southern Whig element has been amply developed by Thomas B. Alexander in three articles: "Whiggery and Reconstruction in Tennessee," *Journal of Southern History* (1950); "Persistent Whiggery in Alabama and the Lower South, 1860–1877," *Alabama Review* (1959); and "Persistent Whiggery in the Confederate

South, 1860–1877," *Journal of Southern History* (1961). But Allen W. Trelease in "Who Were the Scalawags?" *Journal of Southern History* (1963) has, in a highly statistical analysis of southern election records, challenged this contention. Former Whigs, he wrote, contributed significantly to the southern Republican leadership only in Tennessee— one of the states Alexander focused on—North Carolina, and Virginia. "Elsewhere the converse was often true," he concluded, with many scalawags coming from groups that had been strongly Jacksonian Democratic before the war.

The most compelling issue of reconstruction was not political, legal, or economic—it was *racial*. The status of four million former slaves, and by extension that of blacks everywhere in the United States, figures prominently in most of the works cited. Besides studies like Vernon Lane Wharton's, in which the freedman is the central figure of a somewhat larger topic, there are many other works that deal specifically with the race issue. The starting point for any student should be John Hope Franklin's "Reconstruction and the Negro," in *New Frontiers of the American Reconstruction* (1966), a critique whose most cogent point is how little is known. Robert Cruden's *The Negro in Reconstruction* (1969) is a sound study whose brevity recommends it to those looking for an introductory work. In specific areas, Willie Lee Rose's *Rehearsal for Reconstruction: The Port Royal Experiment* (1964) describes the wartime efforts to establish a free economy in the Sea Islands along the South Atlantic coast; Otis A. Singletary's *Negro Militia and Reconstruction* (1957) is the definitive work on a heretofore badly distorted subject; and George R. Bentley's *A History of the Freedmen's Bureau* (1955) is the standard reference for this controversial agency, although it has been somewhat superseded by William S. McFeely's *Yankee Stepfather: General O. O. Howard and the Freedmen* (1968) and Martin Abbott's *The Freedmen's Bureau in South Carolina, 1865–1872* (1967), the latter an example of the kind of work that is needed for each of the other former Confederate states. On the subject of desegregation, of which there was not as much as one might suppose, Louis R. Harlan's "Desegregation in New Orleans Public Schools during Reconstruction," *American Historical Review* (1962), about a city where there was a surprising measure of white compliance, is especially instructive.

The reaction of white America to emancipation was, in many respects, as far-reaching as emancipation itself because it called attention to a basic flaw in American society: the longstanding racial prejudice of whites. Various aspects of this subject are analyzed in Forrest G. Wood's *Black Scare: The Racist Response to Emancipation and Reconstruction* (1968); while Leslie H. Fishel, in "Northern Prejudice and Negro Suffrage, 1865–1870," *Journal of Negro History* (1954), discussed one facet of white racism. The contention that many southern whites sympathized with the freedmen is considered by Guion Griffis Johnson in "Southern Paternalism toward Negroes after Emancipation," *Journal of Southern History* (1957); but most of the research dealing with southern white reactions has revealed violence and lawlessness, not paternalism. Despite the momentous pervasiveness of white racist terrorism in the South during reconstruction, there was no adequate general work on this subject until 1971 when Allen W. Trelease's prizewinning *White Terror: The Ku Klux Klan Conspiracy and Southern Reconstruction* was published. A major reason why it took so long, of course, is the fact that southern terrorism was not the result of a unified movement but was the work of a disjointed collection of many different and far-flung groups and individuals who had in common only a reliance on fear and force. Because of this diversity, Herbert Shapiro's "The Ku Klux Klan during Reconstruction: The South Carolina Episode," *Journal of Negro History* (1964), in which the Klan is exposed as a working partner of the Democratic party in that state, is the kind of work that needs to be done for each southern state. The *legal* reaction to emancipation where a conservative state government gradually codified its white supremacy doctrine (thereby eliminating the need for terrorist groups) is described in Charles E. Wynes's *Race Relations in Virginia, 1870–1902* (1961). As for the reactions of the radicals and other reformers, the student should compare Patrick Riddleberger's "The Radicals' Abandonment of the Negro during Reconstruction," *Journal of Negro History* (1960), which discusses the latent racism of many self-proclaimed friends of the freedmen, with James M. McPherson's excellent study *The Struggle for Equality: Abolitionists and the Negro in the Civil War and Reconstruction* (1964), which points out that most of the old abolitionists deplored the declining public and government interest in guaranteeing the freedman's security.

There are a number of books on special topics that should engage the student's interest. *Pardon and Amnesty under Lincoln and Johnson* (1953) by Jonathan Truman Dorris is a highly detailed analysis of the generally liberal posture taken by both Congress and the administration toward former rebel leaders. The longstanding lack of a study of the role of the federal army in the South has been admirably removed by

James E. Sefton's *The United States Army and Reconstruction, 1865–1877* (1967). Charles H. Coleman's *The Election of 1868: The Democratic Effort to Regain Control* (1933) is still the standard work on that subject, but some of its assumptions are no longer valid and it therefore should be read along with more recent works. The role of an organized religious body is discussed in *Northern Methodism and Reconstruction* (1956) by Ralph E. Morrow, a study that suggests a need for additional research into denominational reform efforts. An excellent work on constitutional change is Joseph B. James's *The Framing of the Fourteenth Amendment* (1956), which should be followed up by reading in works dealing with the later history of the amendment; while William Gillette's *The Right to Vote: Politics and the Passage of the Fifteenth Amendment* (1965) is similarly commendable and more interpretative. The role of the Supreme Court during the Civil War and reconstruction era, usually slighted in general histories of the period, has been admirably presented by Stanley I. Kutler in his *Judicial Power and Reconstruction Politics* (1968). Finally, compare C. Vann Woodward's *Reunion and Reaction: The Compromise of 1877 and the End of Reconstruction* (revised, 1956), the pioneering work that revised the standard view of the end of reconstruction, with Keith Ian Polakoff's *The Politics of Inertia: The Election of 1876 and the End of Reconstruction* (1973), which takes the position that the election of Hayes instead of Tilden was due in large measure to an unwillingness of politicians to make difficult decisions.

INDEX